In Memory of my Parents
Tom & Mary Fewer
late of
"Hillcrest",
Gortmore Drive,
Waterford

Acknowledgments

My thanks are due to many people for help and encouragement, personal, technical and professional, over the past eighteen months during which I have been researching this book. Every person I spoke to went out of their way to provide me with whatever information I needed, and they have my sincere gratitude. My particular thanks go to Marie Fitzpatrick, my brothers Michael and Nicholas, and my sons Greg and Pierre. The first three provided first class support and enthusiasm. Pierre Fewer provided computer skills, while Greg Fewer undertook the most ardous task of all by proof-reading my manuscript. I have also been most fortunate in that my niece Fiona Fewer added her graphic designing skills to the production of the cover.

Others who have been more than helpful with their minds and memories include Michael McNena, Anthony Brophy, Johnnie Furlong, Grace Flanagan, Micky Purcell, Tadgh and Margaret Uí Mhaoileoin, Maurice Connolly, Dermot Power, and the late Paddy Walsh of Ballinkina. I also value the cheerful support given to me by Julian Walton. Thanks are also due to the staff of Waterford Municipal Library and Waterford County Library. Special thanks are due to the staff of Modern Printers, Kilkenny, led by Liam Cody.

I would also like to thank those who kindly provided photographs, including Aileen Hynes, Renee Lumley, Barton Hill, Josephine O'Carroll, Maeve Farrell, Nicholas Fewer and Fintan O'Byrne.

Waterford People

A Biographical Dictionary of Waterford

by
T. N. FEWER

Published By
Ballylough Books
Callaghane, Waterford, Ireland

First Edition

ISBN 0953370402

Copyright © 1998 T. N. Fewer

Published by Ballylough Books
Callaghane, Co. Waterford, Ireland
Phone 00353 51 382538
or 088 - 538145

Printed by Modern Printers, Walkin Street, Kilkenny
Phone 00353 56 21739/21303

PREFACE

The city of Waterford is quite small, with a present population of less than fifty thousand, and for many years up to recent times a population of less than thirty-five thousand.
Yet it can truly claim to be one of the most important cities in Ireland. The city (and county), because of its position on a large navigable river, strategically placed at the South-East corner of Ireland, has been the starting point, both for incoming invasions down through the centuries, and outgoing voyages of commerce or emigration to distant lands. People born in, or associated with, Waterford have also been closely tied to matters of outstanding national importance, from Thomas Francis Meagher and our national flag to John Redmond and the Home Rule movement, on to Richard Mulcahy and the War of Independence. As time has passed on, our famous names have, thankfully, been more associated with victories on track and field or in literature and the theatre rather than in political or military struggle. But whatever the endeavour, there will always be a Waterford connection.

I have always believed that a biographical dictionary of Waterford would be a useful and interesting book to have on the shelves to refer to or 'dip into' from time to time. Although this present book does not make any scholarly claims, every effort has been made to verify the details contained in it. It is however an eclectic collection of the names of just some of the people who, in some interesting or unique way, have touched Waterford as they passed by. I am sure I have missed a few. With apologies, these will have to wait until another day.

T. N. Fewer
Callaghane, Waterford 1998

A

ALCOCK, DEBORAH (d.1913) Daughter of Waterford clergyman, she wrote several novels, the best-known being "The Spanish Brothers".

ALCOCK, Rev. JAMES (1805-1983); Church of Ireland Vicar of Ring, Co. Waterford, for 60 years. During the famine years of 1846 to 1848 he made enormous efforts to help the fishermen of Ring and their families who had reached a state of extreme destitution. As their crops failed they had sold much of their nets and gear to buy food. The Rev. Alcock appealed to the Quakers in Waterford for help and over the next 3 years obtained and administered funding which enabled fishermen to purchase new nets and other fishing gear which literally, in many cases, saved their lives. He believed in the principle of helping people to help themselves rather than direct charity. In 1848-49 a pier was erected at Ballinagoul, Ring at the behest of the Rev. Alcock and the Waterford Quakers. He died in 1893 at the age of 88.

ANDERSON; The name of a well-known family (established at Gracedieu, Co. Waterford since the 17th century) prominent in military and medical circles with several branches which lived in the Waterford area in the latter part of the 19th century and up to recent times. They included Brigadier General Sir Francis Anderson, (1860-1920) of Ballydavid, Woodstown; Lady Ellen Catherine Anderson (1864-1956) of Gracedieu, Tramore Road; her son, Lt.-Col. C.B.C. Anderson, OBE, FRCS, RAMC who died in 1979; Dr. Robert Carew Anderson, (1815-1885) Inspector General of Hospitals, of Suir View, Ferrybank. Other members of the family lived at such well-known houses as Brook Lodge; Prospect, Ferrybank; Ballymountain; and Bellview.

ANDERSON, JULIAN, Born at Gracedieu, Tramore Road, Co. Waterford. Educated at Newtown School. At a very early age he became a keen wind-surfer, sailing out of the Waterford Harbour

Sailing Club in Dunmore East. He went on to become successful in international windsurfing. In Italy in 1987, at the age of 18, he won the Mistral Boardsailing World Championship.

ANTHONY, MARK. (1786-1867) Naval Hero and Harbour-master. Born at Stradbally, Co. Waterford, Mark Anthony joined the Royal Navy in 1801 aboard H.M.S. *Hunter* and first saw action against the French off Cuba. His ability and gallantry in action over the next few years brought him promotion and he took part in the Battle of Trafalgar (1805) as a Commander aboard H.M.S. *Naiad*. After the battle he was congratulated on his service by the Admiralty. Later he served under Captain Beresford (son of the first Marquis of Waterford and later Admiral Sir John Poer Beresford) and saw service in many ships before obtaining the shore post of Harbour Master at Dunmore East which was then the terminus of the Milford mailboat and one of only three ports in Ireland authorized to handle the Royal Mail. However, after a relatively few years the mailboat moved to a base in Waterford city and Captain Anthony retired to his ancestral home at Seafield, where he lived the remainder of his life, it is said, in comparative poverty.

ARMSTRONG, JOHN WARD, (1915-1987) Church of Ireland Bishop of Waterford and Primate of all Ireland. Born on September 30th 1915. Ordained deacon in 1938 and priest in 1939. Made bishop of Cashel , Emly, Waterford and Lismore in 1968, to which the diocese of Ossory, Ferns and Leighlin was added in 1977. On the 25th of February 1980 he was elected Archbishop of Armagh and Primate of All Ireland & Metropolitan. He retired in February 1986, and died on July 25th 1987. He regarded his years in Waterford as amongst the happiest in his life, because "he loved the power of the ecumenical spirit which seemed to flourish there", and he enjoyed a particularly friendly relationship with the Catholic Bishop of Waterford of the time, Dr. Russell. Dr. Armstrong lived in a relatively modest house at Newtown, of which he and his wife, who taught at the Church of Ireland National School (now called Christ Church National School) at Lower Newtown, were very fond. The house was formerly a home of the Strangman family and is now owned by Dr Edward Grant.

ARDAGH, Sir JOHN CHARLES.(1840-1907)   Major-general.
Born at Comeragh, Co. Waterford in 1840. Educated at Trinity
College Dublin and at Woolwich . Entered the Royal Engineers
and saw service in Turkey, Egypt and India. He was present at
the battles of Tel-el-Kebir (1882) and El Teb (1884), and private
secretary to the viceroy of India, 1888-94. Knighted in 1894.
Hon. LL.D, Dublin, 1897. He was married to the Countess of
Malmesbury.

ARRIGAN, THOMAS (died 1972) of Green Street, Waterford,
was captain of the Waterford Soccer Team which, on Sunday,
April 18th 1937, was the first Waterford team to win the
Football Association of Ireland Cup. The game took place at
Dalymount Park, and in front of 35,000 spectators, Waterford
beat St James Gate by 2 goals to 1. The rest of the team
captained by Arrigan were; A. Robinson, H. Foy, J. McDonnell,
W. Walsh, T. Fullerton, J. Phelan, S. Gill, E. Noonan, J.
McGourty and T. O'Keefe. The Waterford goals were scored by
Eugene Noonan on a pass from John McGourty, and Tim O'Keefe
also on a pass from McGourty.

ATHERTON, JOHN (1598 - 1640) Anglican Bishop of Waterford
and Lismore (1636), who, unfortunately for him, had the
temerity to prosecute the Earl of Cork for the recovery of
Ardmore, Lismore and other lands which were formerly the
property of the church. He was made a scapegoat by being
accused of a felony ("of a secret nature") with another man. He
was executed on December 5th 1640. His so-called co-felon and
accuser, when he came to be executed himself, allegedly
confessed to the falseness of his accusation.

AYLWARD, An Anglo-Norman family, thought to have come
from Bristol, which has been prominent in the affairs of
Waterford since the 14th century.

AYLWARD, JOHN   Owner of the castle and estate at Faithlegg
when Cromwell arrived in Ireland (1649). Cromwell had known
Aylward in London and knew he was a Catholic, but in deference
to their former friendship offered to pass him by if he would give
the appearance of accepting the Protestant faith, and supporting

Cromwell. This, Aylward, after reflection, would not do, and so a Captain William Bolton, on Cromwell's instructions, laid siege to the castle, took it, and executed the garrison. The Bolton family remained in posssession of the estate until 1819.

AYLWARD, JOHN (1915-1995) Businessman and entrepreneur, born in Waterford. In the 1930s he worked in the mining industry in Australia. Returned to Waterford. Founder of many businesses in the city including (1938) a wholesale grocery and confectionery which later (1960) was reputed to be the first Cash & Carry outside Dublin. In 1940 he organised the manufacture of charcoal for fuel for goods vehicles during WW11. Founding director of Southern Refrigeration, 1948. Founder of Snowcream Waterford, in 1952, he later founded Snowcream Wexford and Snowcream Midlands.

AYLWARD, PETER Mayor of Waterford, (1566 - 1567), was a merchant and property owner. He owned substantial property in Passage and built a tower house there which was demolished in the 17th century. His coat of arms still exists, embedded in the rock, but largely hidden from view by a nineteenth century building opposite the Post Office. He died in 1594.

AYLWARD, Sir RICHARD (1540 - 1626) Son of Peter. Mayor of Waterford. Became a freeman of the city in 1573, and a member of parliament for Waterford in 1585. He first became Mayor of Waterford in 1592. He had inherited wealth and property and added to it during his lifetime . Became involved in contentious legal battles, especially with the equally prominent Sherlock family, which lasted up to and beyond his death. He was sheriff of Waterford in 1599, and mayor again in 1605/06, 1606/07 and 1616/17. He held on to these posts by becoming , in public at least, a Protestant, and in 1602 he was knighted for his services by Lord Mountjoy. He was not altogether popular with the Waterford people, but they continued to elect him on the basis that, as a kind of palace pet, he might keep them out of harm, and he was the only one who would take the oath of allegiance. (ref. Eamonn McEneaney)

B

BACIK, CHARLES (1910-1991) Founder of the modern Waterford Glass. Born near Prague, Czechoslovakia, Charles Bacik was, at the time of the Communist take-over of his country, a successful businessman with several glass factories in operation. Unwilling to accept a life under communism he fled to Ireland, arriving in Waterford with his wife and three children in 1946. Using mainly borrowed funds, the new Waterford Glass, with a capital of IR15,000.00, started production in 1947. In the same year, Miroslav Havel, a skilled glass engraver, joined him from from Prague. Unfortunately, technical problems (the first furnace blew up) and lack of capital pushed the company to the brink. Approaches from Joe McGrath of the Irish Glass Bottle Co. were at first rejected by Bacik, but increasing debts led to the takeover of Waterford Glass by McGrath in 1950. Financial and technical support was now available in abundance and by 1952 Waterford Crystal products were being distributed world-wide. Bacik's position with the new owners was uncertain for several years. Although they wanted his expertise they did not offer him an official position until the mid fifties. In 1947 Charles Bacik, with the co-operation of VEC, set up a course of study in glass technology. "It was a deliberate attempt to provide his workers with a sound technical foundation as well as to instill an apppreciation of glass as an art form" (J.M.Hearne, Decies No.50) Charles Bacik lived for a time in Grange Park, Waterford, but in later life moved to Piltown, Co. Kilkenny, where he died in 1991.

BACKAS, Members of the Backas family were prominent in Waterford in the 17th, 18th, and 19th centuries. In 1698 Robert Backas was nominated for the post of high constable of the city. His descendant, George, was an alderman in Waterford from 1750 to 1771 and owned considerable property in the city. His son, Robert, who was a lieutenant in Col. William Alcock's regiment of foot in 1756, went on to become a man of property and 'one of the oldest common councilmen' of Waterford. In 1798 he leased Butlerstown Castle and although he died in 1813 the castle remained in his family until 1870, when it was sold to Samuel Ferguson.

BARKER, FRANCIS. (1773-1859) Physician. Born in Waterford. Educated at Trinity College Dublin (B.A. 1793 and M.D. 1810) and Edinburgh University where he was a friend of Sir Walter Scott. On his return to Waterford he opened Ireland's first fever hospital. Later he settled in Dublin where he was senior physician at Cork Street Hospital (1804) and professor of chemistry at TCD (1808-1850). Founded the first Irish medical journal. Published "Fevers in Ireland"; Editor " Dublin Pharmacopoeia" 1826. Died in Dublin.

BARKER, SAMUEL Mayor of Waterford (1737,1741 and 1753). M.P. for Waterford from 1746 to 1768. His grandfather, Francis and his father, also Francis, had both been mayors before him. During the mayoralties of the Barkers Waterford saw a number of improvements in the facilities of the city. Wooden pipes brought water to a number of private houses and public troughs. The use of slate or stone for roofing instead of the commonly used thatch was encouraged, to help prevent fires. A system of street lighting was introduced, using 200 oil-lamps in wall brackets, and several new public buildings were erected, including a jail, a courthouse (designed by James Gandon, but demolished in the 19th century) and an Exchange, where merchants met to trade and exchange business contracts. Samuel Barker's house, on the hillside between Ballybricken and the River Suir, posessed a marvelous garden described by Charles Smith as: " beautifully cut into slopes and terrace walks at the bottom of which is a handsome canal with other reservoirs higher up. In the lower canal are fountains which play to a considerable height, the side of which is beautified with statues standing in niches." The garden also included a romantic gothic arch (the ruins of St Thomas's chapel), an aviary, ponds stocked with carp and tench, and a deer park "stocked with deer of several colours". The gardens are long since gone but the name lives on in Barker Street. (ref. Eamonn McEneaney)

BARRETT, MAURICE PATRICK (1900-1990) Christian brother and religious leader, he was born in Waterford (Lower Yellow Road) in March, 1990 and educated at De La Salle School, Stephen Street. In 1916 he entered the order of St John of God at Stillorgan and began working with mental patients. He then moved to the order's houses in France and was professed as Brother Matthias in 1921. In 1951 he founded the religious order of the Little Brothers of the Good Shepherd to look after the poor and homeless. In 1984 the Freedom of the City of Waterford was conferred on him by Waterford Corporation. He died in New Mexico in 1990.

BARRON, EDWARD, D.D. (1801-1854) Churchman. Born Ballyneale, Co. Waterford. Taught Hebrew and French at St John's College, Waterford. Vicar General of Philadelphia, U.S.A., Bishop of Constantia and Vicar-Apostolic of New Guinea. Died in Savannah, USA.

BARRON, Sir HENRY WINSTON, Bart (1795 - 1872) Eldest son of Pierce Barron of Glenanna, near Dungarvan, Co. Waterford. MP for Waterford, 1832-41, 1848-52, (in this election Thomas Francis Meagher was defeated) and 1865-68. Created baronet in 1841. His son, the second and last baronet, Sir Henry Page-Turner Barron, C.M.G., (1824 - 1900) was born at Belmont Park, Ferrybank, and had a distinguished career in the British diplomatic service. He donated and bequeathed large sums of money to St John's Church, Waterford, and the monument to his father in that church is the only one of it's kind there. He left £6,000 pounds (about £500,000 in present values) for the erection of a new church at Ferrybank and a further £3,000 for the erection of a family mausoleum adjoining it. The Catholic Bishop of the time, Bishop Brownrigg, did not like the idea of the mausoleum and it was never built, the money instead being funnelled into the construction of a special stone-vaulted chapel currently called the Chapel of the Blessed Sacrament. The remaining family of the Barrons, which now resided in England, had nothing further to do with the Ferrybank church and apparently no Barron was ever buried there.

BARRON, PHILLIP F. (1801-1860) Founder of the Irish College,

Seafield, Bonmahon, Co. Waterford. Born at Durrow House. Educated at Trinity College, but left after three years without taking a degree. Bought the *"Waterford Chronicle"* newspaper (1825). Supported Henry Villiers Stuart against Lord George Beresford in the 1826 election. Unable to pay his debts, he fled to France and then to Italy. While on the continent he became aware of the importance of the culture, music, songs and languages of the different countries he visited and returned to Ireland determined to open a school which would teach Irish language and culture. He contacted scholars all over the country and gained some support. Building of a college commenced (c.1834) on a site leased from Peter Anthony in Seafield. It opened on Jan 1st 1835 with an ambitious curriculum which included, Irish, mathematics, navigation, history, Latin, Greek and Hebrew. Sadly, the mortgage was foreclosed after nine months, and Philip Barron fled once more to France, where he died in 1860. In the 1830s he had also begun publication of *"Ancient Ireland"*, which was to have been a monthly publication, but only the first volume was printed.

BELL, HENRY (1838-1922) Chemist. Born in Lisburn, he moved to Cork as a child with his Quaker parents. Later he moved to Waterford and opened a chemist's shop on the Quay beside the Granville Hotel. The shop later became a kind of landmark for children who used to gaze in awe at a huge gilded 'bell' which hung outside over the door, and which, at Christmas time, used to be decorated with lights. Henry married Anna Jane Davis. Their children, Albert, Anna and Frederick attended Newtown School. In their adult life they became deeply interested in the care and welfare of the poor and homeless. Albert became involved, with the approval of the Waterford Quaker community, in the opening of several 'Tuskar' lodging-houses which gave cheap accomodation to homeless men during the nineteen-twenties and thirties. He died in 1912, aged 48. Anna and Frederick were largely responsible for the Munster Dining Rooms (off Henrietta Street in Waterford) which provided good, hot, and healthy meals for four pence. These charitable meals were partly funded by an adjoining café with good furnishings, tablecloths etc., which served the passerby at more commercial rates, although the food was basically the same. The Munster Rooms, which closed in 1935, also sold tokens to their supporters, who gave them to street beggars, thereby ensuring that the recipients got fed rather than drunk. Anna Bell died in 1937 at the age of 67, and Frederick died in 1941 at the age of 69. Towards the end of the 1930s Bell's Chemist Shop was taken over by Arthur Westcott-Pitt (q.v.) and his brother, who were related to the Bells. They produced a number of patent medicines in a small factory behind the Ulster Bank building on the Quay. Competition from modern mass-production closed this business and the chemist's shop in the early 1950s.

BERESFORD, LORD GEORGE (d.1839) Fourth son of the first Marquis of Waterford, he is best remembered as the representative of the powerful Beresford family who stood for election to the British Parliament in 1826, with every expectation of being elected as a matter of form, by an electorate composed to a significant degree, of tenants of the Marquis. He was opposed and defeated by Henry Villiers Stuart (q.v.), who was supported by fellow liberal Protestants such as Sir Richard Musgrave, and wealthy and influential Catholics including the Meaghers and Gallweys.

BERESFORD, Sir John Poer (1766-1844) Admiral, illegitimate son of George de la Poer Beresford (afterwards Marquis of Waterford). Joined the navy in 1782, and by 1795 had reached the rank of captain. Successfully engaged the French at Hampton Roads in 1795. Commanded the blockade of Lorient, 1808-09; Senior Officer off Brest , 1810; in North Sea, 1811, and on American coast, 1812-14. Commanded the *Royal Sovereign* yacht, 1814. Baronet and rear-admiral, 1814, KCB, 1819; commanded at Leith, 1820-23; and at Nore, 1830-33; vice-admiral, 1821, Admiral, 1838. Represented various constituencies at Westminster from 1812 to 1835.

BERESFORD, WILLIAM CARR, (1768-1854), general; illegitimate son of George de la Poer Beresford, Marquis of Waterford. At the age of seventeen entered a military school at Strasburg and in a wide-ranging military career he rose from ensign (1785) to Lieutenant-Colonel in command of the

Connaught Rangers in the conquest of the West Indies and to Major-general, (1808) and was then made marshall in the Portugese army. Re-organised the Portugese army (1809). Served in Nova Scotia, Toulon, Corsica, the West Indies, Jersey, India, Egypt, Buenos Aires, Madeira, Portugal, Italy and France. Defeated Marshall Soult at Albuera (1811). For this and other services he was knighted and received the thanks of Parliament. Was at Badajoz and was severely wounded at Salamanca. In 1814 he was created Baron, Lord Beresford of Albuera and Cappoquin, and in 1823 Viscount Beresford. General, 1825; Master-general of Ordinance, 1828-30. His conduct at Albuera was criticised by Colonel Napier (Beresford had allowed Marshall Soult to outmanoeuvre him "and by all the laws of war was utterly beaten" before a superhuman effort drove Soult from the field, but at a cost of 4,100 casualties out of the British contingent of 8,000). Beresford published pamphlets in his own defense.

BERESFORD, Sir CHARLES WILLIAM de la POER, 1st Baron (1846-1919) Admiral; son of 4th marquis of Waterford. Joined navy in 1859, reached rank of captain 1882. Served at Alexandria and on the Nile Expedition (1884). A lord of the Admiralty (1886-1888) he resigned to sit as a Conservative MP. Commanded Mediterranean Fleet (1905-1907), Channel Fleet (1907-1909). A "trenchant" naval critic, he published his "Memoirs" in 1914.

BIANCONI, CHARLES (1786-1875) Born in Italy, he came to Ireland in 1802 as an apprentice to Andrea Faroni, a seller of prints and statuettes. He and other young boys were employed selling Faroni's wares in the area of Waterford and Wexford. After a couple of years he went into business on his own account, establishing himself in Carrick-on-Suir in 1806 and a year or two later in Clonmel. He became a great friend and admirer of Edmund Rice who had given him help and advice when he first arrived in Ireland. In later years he sent Rice £50 each year and made arrangements to bequeath his fortune to him if he died without issue. On his travels he noted the lack of any form of reliable transport and in 1815, when he had saved some capital, and when there were plenty of cheap horses available due to the end of the Napoleonic wars, he started his first one-horse stage car service between Clonmel and Cahir. Each car carried six passengers and their luggage and the venture was so successful that within a few years Bianconi 'long' cars, (some of these carried 18 or twenty passengers and were drawn by four horses) could be seen plying their trade between most of the market towns in the south and west of Ireland. At one time his vehicles were daily travelling almost 4,000 miles in twenty-two different counties and annual fares totalled £40,000.00. He became a wealthy man, and bought an estate on the banks of the Suir in Tipperary called Longfield House. Waterford was an important terminus for his cars, and passengers were picked up or dropped off at the Commins Commercial Hotel, which Bianconi had purchased from the Meagher family, and which is now the Granville Hotel. In 1865 he sold the business to his employees and retired to his salmon beat at Longfield where he died in September 1875, aged 89.

BLAKE, JOHN A. (1826-1887) Mayor of Waterford 1855 to 1858 and M.P. for Waterford, 1857-1859. Inspector of Fisheries. Helped found the *"Waterford Citizen"* newspaper. Was mainly responsible for the establishment of the "People's Park", and for the opening up of Broad Street. He married Adelaide Power, daughter of Nicholas Power of Faithlegge. Died in London and was buried at Kensal Green Cemetery.

BOATE, EDWARD, WELLINGTON (1822-1871) Journalist, born in Waterford, son of George Boate of H.M. Customs & Excise. Edited the *Waterford Chronicle* and the *Wexford Guardian*. Reported in House of Commons for *The Times*. Emigrated to the U.S.. During the American Civil War he joined the 42nd Battalion, New York Volunteers. Taken prisoner and sent to Belle Island. Married Henrietta Bruce O'Neill of Twie Castle, Donegal, in 1848. Died in Philadelphia. The Boate family used to be prominent in the Dungarvan area where they were substantial land owners. (Ref. Decies XL111.)

BOLTON FAMILY. William and Thomas Bolton were both officers in Cromwell's army which invaded Waterford in 1649. William ended up with Faithlegg (see John Aylward) and

Thomas established Mount Bolton . When Charles 11 came to
the throne, they both readily switched their alliegance to him,
were pardoned, and held on to their lands.   In due course
William became a freeman of the city, an alderman, mayor and
high sheriff, but never lost his dislike of Catholics or dissenters
of any kind. William's great-grandson Cornelius (c.1714 - 1778),
despite a challenge to his legitimacy by his Mount Bolton
cousins, inherited Faithlegg. He married the sister of Samuel
Barker and became successfully involved in local politics, being
mayor of Waterford in 1743-1744 and again in 1761-1762. In
1769 he succeeded Samuel Barker as M.P. for Waterford.

BOLTON, CORNELIUS (1751-1829)
Great-great-grandson of William, and son of Cornelius (above),
carried on the role of the Bolton family in politics, becoming M.P.
for Waterford from 1776 to 1783, and mayor of Waterford (1810-
1811 and 1816-17).   He was also a progressive farmer and was
highly praised by Arthur Young (q.v.). He built Faithlegg House,
one of the finest mansions in the county, in the 1780s. He made
a number of ventures into manufacturing, especially in the
cotton industry, and brought miners over from Wales to dig
exploratory shafts on his land, but these ventures proved to be
expensive and a drain on capital, and like "many other projected
attempts by the same spirited individual were, unhappily for the
country, unsuccessful" (Ryland). In 1819 he was forced to sell
Faithlegg to Nicholas Power.   For a time though, Bolton's
Landing, as Cheekpoint was known at the time, was a hive of
activity, with factories, fish packing stations and regular sailing
connections to England and Wales. Cornelius Bolton also built
a fine hotel in Cheekpoint but various travellers wrote such
embarrassing reports about the slovenly service there that it too
closed down!   Around 1820 he retired to Belmont House,
Cappoquin (the home of his son-in-law, Pierce Barron) where he
died in 1829. Rather like Ozymandias, very little remains of
Bolton's empire to-day, but an ancient milestone, set in the wall
at "Weston", on Newtown Road, tells the distance to Passage and
Bolton's Landing. One other milestone (indicating Bolton)
existed on the left-hand side of the road just past the Island
Lane (where the Maxol Service Station is now) but it
disappeared during road widening in 1997. Bolton Street in

Waterford city is named after his family. The Mount Bolton branch of the family were last recorded living in Brook Lodge in the 1920s. (ref . H. F. Morris)

BOLTON, Capt. WILLIAM (see Aylward, John)

BONAPARTE-WYSE, NAPOLEON ALFRED (1822-1895) (Younger son of Sir Thomas Wyse and Laetitia Bonaparte), High Sheriff of Waterford in 1870.

BONAPARTE - WYSE, WILLIAM CHARLES (1826-1892) Poet and writer, (son of Sir Thomas Wyse and Laetitia Bonaparte, niece of the Emperor Napoleon), High Sheriff of Waterford 1855: Published (1868) *"Parpaioun Blu"* (lyrics in Provencal) and other writings.

BOWYER, BRENDAN Singer, born in Waterford Oct. 1938, and educated at Waterpark College. Coming from a musical background, he started singing in his teens and joined the Royal Showband in 1957. His speciality was rock 'n' roll and his athletic performances on stage brought the huge dancing crowds to a halt. He was probably Ireland's biggest pop-music star of the sixties. His rendition of the "Hucklebuck" is still popular today. In 1971 he left the Royal Showband and began a long-standing annual residency in Las Vegas with his new band, the Big Eight, returning each year for a tour of Ireland.

BOWYER, STANLEY (1910-1980) Musician, music teacher, talented and popular organist and choir-master at the Catholic Cathedral, Waterford. Father of Brendan Bowyer. Born in Blackpool, only child of Albert and Olive (Wentwood) Bowyer. His parents were both musicians (his mother was also a well-known contralto) and they travelled all over England with their own "Bowyer-Wentworth Opera Company" putting on "IL TRAVATORE", Wallace's "MARITANA", and other operas. Stanley's mother was an accomplished pianist and provided the musical background for silent films, sometimes accompanied by her small son on the violin. Stanley Bowyer was organist in the Redemptionist Church in Limerick before moving to Waterford and marrying Maura Daniels of Dunmore East. They lived in

Bailey's New Street and for many years owned and operated the Steamship Bar there, although Stanley is said to have disliked the bar and preferred teaching and playing music. He was organist at the Dominican Church for some time before going to the Cathedral. He taught music at several schools, including Waterpark College, De La Salle College, the Ursuline Convent and Sacred Heart of Mary Convent, Ferrybank. The author remembers him as a good-natured, enthusiastic teacher, patiently trying to instill the rudiments of the barcarolle into a class at Waterpark. He was the first Musical Director of the Waterford International Festival of Light Opera, a position into which he put enormous effort; at one time burning the midnight oil to write the full score, in all its parts, for the orchestra. Maura died in the early seventies. He later married May Kelly, and they had five years of happiness before he died in 1980.

BOYLE, ROBERT (1627-1691) Philosopher and scientist. Born Jan. 25th 1627 at Lismore Castle, Co. Waterford. Sent to Eton at an early age and then travelled extensively on the continent, becoming fluent in French and Italian. Lived in Dorset for some years before moving to London in 1668 where he quickly became a leading member of the scientific and philosophical community. A founding member of the Royal Society, he began to publish the findings of his experiments, particularily the properties of air, in 1660. He is best known for his famous "Boyle's Law" which says that the volume of a gas at constant temperature, varies inversely to the pressure applied to the gas. He also investigated vacuums, air and its relationship to the transmission of sound; the refraction of light; electricity and colour. He was a devoutly religious man, and had Bibles printed and distributed at his own expense. He commissioned *Bedell's Irish Bible*, which was published in 1686. He never married and died in London having refused a peerage and many other honours.

BRENAN, EDWARD (fl. 1859) of Dungarvan Co. Waterford. Local naturalist and historian. In 1859 he read a paper to the Royal Dublin Society to publicise the finding, in a limestone quarry at Shandon, of fossilised remains of "mammoth, bear, rein-deer, hare and horse".

BRENAN, R. EDMOND (1846-1917) In 1869, R. E. Brenan, postmaster of Dungarvan, Co. Waterford, won what is believed to have been the first cycle-race for a Challenge Cup held in this country, or possibly any other country. In the same year the first cycling club in Ireland was founded : the Dungarvan Ramblers C.C.

BRENNAN, Dr THOMAS (1924 - 1998) Politician. Born in Ferrybank, Nov 24th, 1924. Educated at Ferrybank CBS and De La Salle College. Worked for most of his life for Coras Iompar Éireann. Was chairman of the Waterford Branch of the ITGWU in 1956, and a member of the Waterford Council of Trade Unions from 1950 to 1966. Elected to Waterford Corporation for the Labour Party in 1960 and was re-elected repeatedly until his retirement. Mayor of Waterford 1963-64, 1973-74 and 1980-81. Although a popular public representative, he was unsuccessful in his attempts to be elected to the Dail. He was an active member of many local charitable organisations and was a member of the Board of Governors of Waterford County and City Infirmary, University College Dublin and University College Cork. He served on the Finance Committee of UCD for three terms and was a member of the Senate of N.U.I. In recognition of his services, the National University of Ireland conferred on him an honorary doctorate. He was a member of Waterford Vocational Education Committee for ten years and Vice-President of Waterford Literary and Historical Society. He has been one of the longest serving members in recent times of the Waterford Harbour Commissioners of which he was chairman for several terms since 1986 . In 1950 he married Stella Tyrell of Johnstown. He died in March 1998.

BROPHY, ANTHONY (b. 1941) Businessman, music lover and freelance writer. Born at Newtown, Waterford City. Raised at the family home in Lombard Street. Educated at Waterpark. Studied accountancy. Worked at Waterford Glass (1965-1989) where he became a director. On a flight to the USA in 1989 he conceived the idea of a music society on a grand scale, i.e., that would encourage symphony orchestras to visit Waterford. For some years Waterford had been a backwater in this regard and the RTE Symphony Orchestra had not visited the city in almost

20 years. On his return, he formed, with Eric de Courcy, Larry O'Sullivan , Simon Harrison, Colin Chapman, and others, the Symphony Club of Waterford, (affectionately known as "SCOW"). The first concert was in May 1989 and the visitors were The Royal Philharmonic Orchestra conducted by Sir Charles Groves. They first played "Dance Music" by Eric Sweeney, the Head of the Music Department of WIT, and then the celebrated Irish pianist John O'Conor played Beethoven's Third Piano Concerto. This was followed by Tchaikovsky's Fifth Symphony. The concert was a resounding success with a full house. This success has continued over the past eight seasons during which time SCOW has presented some forty concerts at various venues before settling in its permanent home at the College Hall of WIT, under the close supervision of its present chairman, Eric Sweeney. Always fascinated by the sea, and at one time Shipping Correspondent for *The Munster Express*, writing under the name of "Neptune", Anthony Brophy was also one of the main movers in the bringing of cruise liners to Waterford which has become such a success story.

BROWNE, NOEL, TD (1915-1997) Doctor and politician, born Co.Waterford Dec 20th 1915. Ed. CBS Ballinrobe and England, qualified as doctor at TCD. Having suffered from TB he became a campaigner for its eradication. Joined Clann na Poblachta, elected to Dail in 1948, Minister for Health 1948 - 1951. As Minister for Health one of his first acts was to liquidate the department's assets, which amounted to almost £20 million in investments and bonds. With this money, and £10 million borrowed on the strength of future income from the Irish Sweep Stakes, he embarked on a programme of building hospitals with the express aim of removing TB from Ireland. Many of these hospitals were in fact purpose-built sanatoria such as Ardkeen Hospital, with totally independent single-story buildings as seperate wards. This dramatic action, a huge leap in the medical history of Ireland, with the aid of new drugs, virtually eliminated tuberculosis and must be considered his greatest achievement. Later he became involved in conflict with the Roman Catholic Church over his "Mother and Child" scheme which would have provided free prenatal and postnatal medical services. The hierarchy would not tolerate anything to do with what they regarded as socialism. To avoid a row with the Church the cabinet withdrew support and his party leader, Sean McBride, asked him to resign, stating; "The creation of a situation where it is made to appear that a conflict exists between the spiritual and temporal authorities is always undesirable ; in the case of Ireland it is highly damaging to the cause of national unity and should have been avoided". Later he was elected a TD under various banners: Fianna Fail, Labour, and as an Independent. He co-founded the National Progresssive Democrats and served in the Dail for them. He was regarded by some as a man before his time and by others as a loose cannon, a socialist radical, a man who found it difficult to submit to party disipline. In 1977 he broke away from the NPDs and then co-founded the Socialist Labour Party. While with the Labour Party (1969-73) he introduced the first family planning bill in the Dail. He wrote a successful autobiography, "Against the Tide", in 1986, (on the publication of which, Sean MacBride remarked that it was a pity that "his pastime was to fire so many poisoned arrows".) He died in 1997.

BROWNE, PATRICK, TD. Elected Fianna Fail TD in 1966 and 1969, lost his seat in election of 1973. He was also mayor of Waterford from 1953 to 1955, and from 1964 to 1967.

BRUGHA, CATHAL (1874-1922) Republican revolutionary born in Dublin as Charles William St John Burgess. Educated at Belvedere College. Lieutenant, Irish Volunteers 1913. Served under Eamonn Ceannt in the 1916 Rising, and was severely wounded. Chief of Staff, IRA, 1917 to 1919, then Minister for Defence. Presided at first meeting of the Dail (in the absence of De Valera and Griffith who were both in prison) on Jan 21st 1919. Was first TD to represent Waterford in Dail Eireann (1918-1922). Opposed the Treaty of 1922 and fought on the republican side in the 1922-23 Civil War. Died of wounds received in the fighting in O'Connell Street, Dublin.

BUGGY, PADDY (b. 1929) All-Ireland Hurler and President of the GAA. His father was from Three Castles, Kilkenny but moved to Slieverue where Paddy spent much of his childhood. Although he attended Mount Sion CBS, he joined Slieverue

GAA club and went on to become a member of the Kilkenny All-Ireland team which, ironically, was beaten by Waterford in 1959. He won numerous awards including 5 Leinster Championship Medals. He also played inter-provincial college hurling with Munster. One of his favourite memories is of being captain of the Mount Sion CBS team which won the inter-schools Hackett Cup. He was a fast and skillful player with a deep sense of sportmanship which won him the respect of all those he played for or against. Perhaps because of this and his own hard work he rose in the ranks of the GAA, becoming President in its centenary year in 1984. In the same year he was conferred with an honorary doctorate by the N.U.I. He has lived at Marymount, Ferrybank since 1958, and is an active member of Waterford Golf Club.

BULBULIA, Catherine, (b.1943) Politician and administrator. Born in Dublin. Educated at the Sacred Heart of Mary Convent, Ferrybank, Waterford, College of Catering, Cathal Brugha Street, Dublin and UCD. A founder member of the Waterford branch of the Women's Political Association. An aquaintance and admirer of Garret Fitzgerald when in UCD, she became a member of Fine Gael when he became party leader. Elected Waterford C.C. in 1979 (first woman elected) with huge majority. Failed to be nominated as Dail candidate in 1981 election but was made a candidate by FG headquarters. However the votes of 1979 did not materialize and she did not win a seat. Member of the Senate 1981-89. Executive Director, Waterford Chamber of Commerce 1991-1997 when she resigned to contest the general election on behalf of the Progressive Democrats but failed to win a seat. After the election she secured the position of principle advisor and manager to Mary Harney, TD, leader of the Progressive Democrats and Táiniste in the new government. Founder member of OASIS (the shelter for victims of domestic violence) and director of Waterford Childcare.

BURKITT, Dr ROBERT J. (1807-1893) Physician and ornithologist. Practised as a physician in Waterford for most of his life, but had a "life-long devotion to ornithology". He added the Barred Warbler to the list of rare birds that visit Ireland, and made numerous contributions to Irish ornitholigical

records.   He made donations of rare birds to the National
Museum and to Trinity College, the most famous of these
donations being the only specimen of Great Auk found in Irish
waters. The entry in his collecting book states; "Sept. 7th 1834.
I obtained a young Penguin from Francis Davis Esq.,, which
was taken off Ballymacaw several miles west of Waterford
Harbour & which I presented to the Museum of Trinity College,
Dublin, 1844". R. J. Ussher, the ornithologist and writer,
referred to him in *"The Irish Naturalist"* (No. 2, p224) as being
of " singular sincerity and simplicity of character". He retired
to Belmullet in 1883 and died in 1893. (Ref. Fergus J. O'Rourke)

BURTCHALL, HENRIETTA In her will dated 1822 she left
money for the erection of a home for the "support of poor
Protestants". A building was duly erected at Beresford Street
(now Parnell Street) and still provides accomodation for elderly
ladies (not necessarily of the Protestant faith).

BUTLER, JOHN, Labour TD for Waterford, 1923-1927,
contested 1927 election as an Independent but was defeated.
Member WCC 1929 - 34. Joined Fine Gael and was unsuccessful
candidate in elections of 1937 and 1943. Member of Senate from
1939 to 1957 and from 1961 to 1965. His son, Pierce Butler,
became a Senator in 1969.

BUTLER, MATTHEW, (1874-1964)   Historian who, almost
single-handedly, it is said, ran the Waterford Historical Society
in the 1930s. He lived as a child in Corballymore and attended
the Summerville National School for boys.   In his long life he
wrote much about his beloved city and county, including; "A
History of the Barony of Gaultier" (1913), "Waterford; An
Illustrated Guide to City and County" and "Fifty Golden Years;
a history of the Gaelic League in Waterford" (1944).

C

CAMPION, MARIA (1775-1803) Actress, born in Waterford, who first appeared at the Crow Street Theatre, Dublin, in 1792, and rapidly became the heroine of the Irish stage. Appeared at Covent Garden, London, under the name of Mrs Spenser in 1797. Became the second wife of the poet Alexander Pope in 1798. While playing Desdemona at Drury Lane on June 10th 1803, she was taken ill, and died on June 18th. She is buried in Westminster Abbey.

CARACCIOLO, DON NICCOLO d'ARDIA, (1941-1989) Artist. Niccolo Caracciolo was born in what is now Waterford Castle, on Little Island, near Waterford City. His father was a prince and a descendant of Prince Francesco Caracciolo (1752-99), a Neapolitan admiral who had been summarily hanged from the yardarm by Nelson in an incident which aroused more bitter and prolonged controversy than any other in Nelson's life. Niccolo's father married Mary Augusta De Lisle Cecilia Fitzgerald who became heiress to the island on the death of her only brother Patrick (killed at sea while serving with the Royal Navy) in 1943. Niccolo Caracciolo was educated at Waterpark College in the late Forties and early Fifties. In 1952 the family moved to their Dublin home, The Park, Rathfarnham , and Niccolo was sent to school in England before studying art in Florence. He exhibited regularly with the Royal Academy in London and with the Royal Hibernian Academy, of which he was voted a full academician in 1983. He held regular exhibitions in Suzanne MacDougald's Solomon Gallery in the Powerscourt Centre, Dublin. He was killed in a car crash in Italy in 1989. At the time of his death he had built a reputation not only as a painter of landscapes in the classical style, but also as a superb portrait painter. (ref. C. Wilkinson)

CAREW, JOHN EDWARD, (1785-1868) Sculptor, Born in Tramore, he moved to London and became assistant to Sir

Richard Westmacott (1809-23) and was employed by the third Earl of Egremont, a famous patron of the arts, at his estate at Petworth from 1823 to 1837. Spent the latter part of his life in London, where he exhibited at the Royal Academy. He is also thought to have been one of the sculptors who created the four scenes, in bronze, on the base of Nelson's Column in Trafalgar Square. These scenes depict "The Battle of the Nile", "The Battle of St. Vincent", "The Battle of Copenhagen", and "The death of Nelson". Carew died on November 30th 1868 and is buried in Kensal Green Cemetry.

CAREW, ROBERT THOMAS (1747-1834) of Ballinamona, Co. Waterford. High Sheriff, 1779. In 1771 he married Frances, daughter of Thomas Boyse of Bishop's Hall, Co. Kilkenny, and lived at Snowhill for a time before inheriting the family estate at Ballinamona. His descendant, Major R. Carew, was a well-liked old gentleman who died in the late Seventies. He is remembered for his great interest in motor cars and mechanical matters generally. He is thought to have been one of the first farmers in the Waterford area to use a combine harvester. His only child, a daughter, who was christened Una but changed her name to Roberta, married a Mr Parkes and moved to London, where she died c. 1989. Another branch of the Carew family lived at Woodstown House, including Robert Shapland Carew, who represented Waterford in the Irish Parliament of 1784.

CARROLL, STANISLAUS J., (STAN) (1907-1986) Waterford Borough Surveyor and local historian. Born in Bellgrove House, Monkstown, Co. Dublin on Jan 2nd 1907. Studied at Trinity (BA, BAI) and worked for Dun Laoghaire Corporation and Dublin Corporation before being appointed Engineer at Galway in 1942. In 1948 he applied for and won the post of Borough Surveyor (later the position became City Engineer) with Waterford Corporation. Moved to Waterford and stayed for a while with his cousin Capt. Desmond Carroll, harbourmaster at Dunmore East before moving into Ardaun, Newtown. He remained with Waterford Corporation until his retirement in 1973 after which he was appointed an inspector for An Bord Pleanála. He was deeply interested in history, and was a founder member of the Old Galway Society, a member of the Military History Society and the Old Dublin Society, and a committee member of the Group for the Study of Irish Historic Settlement. His greatest committment was, however , to the Old Waterford Society, to which he gave years of service and support, filling at different times the positions of honorary secretary, honorary editor, vice-chairman and chairman. He contributed many papers and articles, on a variety of subjects, all of which had the hall-mark of meticulous research. Stan Carroll's greatest contribution to Waterford was The Waterford Room in the City Library. This is an archive of books, articles and papers devoted to Waterford's history in all spheres of life, and which was established under his urging and guidance.

CARROLL, WILLIAM (Bill) A resident of Tramore, he was founding chairman, in 1958, of the Waterford International Festival of Light Opera. The first executive committee of the Festival were; Bill Carroll (chairman), George Goodfellow, Joe O'Regan, Michael Browne, Liam Doody, Ronnie Milne, John McNamara, Stanley Bowyer, C.V. Kavanagh, Tom Moylan, Gerry O'Donoghue, Jim Conway, Barry Limmond and Josephine Moylan. The first ever performance at the Festival was "The White Horse Inn" by the Garan-Coe-Garwen (Wales) singers, on September 4th 1959.

CARTHAGE, SAINT
St Carthage founded a monastery at Lismore in the 7th Century. "The monastery soon grew to be a great school, to which students and religious came from all parts of Ireland, and some from beyond the seas. Its bishops, abbots, anchorites and teachers are referred to over and over again in the Irish annals." (Canon Power)

CARVER, RICHARD (1683-1754) Artist. Born in Waterford, and sent to Bluecoat School, Dublin, in 1697. Became landscape and historical painter (there is believed to be an altar painting by him in Waterford). Died suddenly in 1754. His son, Robert Carver (c.1750-1791) born in Dublin, studied painting under Robert West, and became scene painter for Smock Alley and Crow Street Theatres. In 1769 he was invited to London by the famous actor and producer David Garrick to be principle scene

painter in the Drury Lane Theatre. The Dublin actor Spranger
Barry also worked at Drury Lane, and when he quarrelled with
Garrick and moved to Covent Garden Robert Carver went with
him and worked there until his death at 13 Bow Street, Covent
Garden, in November 1791. He exhibited at the Royal Academy
in 1789 and 1790.

CASHMAN, DENIS B. (1840-1897) Born in Waterford. Trained
in law before joining the local branch of the Fenians. Arrested in
Dublin and sentenced to seven years penal servitude. When
released went to America and became associated with John
Boyle O'Reilly on *"The Boston Pilot"*. Published "Life of Michael
Davitt". Died in Brooklyn, New York in 1897.

CAVANAGH, MICHAEL, (1822-1892) Born in Cappoquin, Co.
Waterford. Supported Young Ireland movement. Follower of
Thomas Francis Meagher. Participated in attack on Cappoquin
Barracks in 1849 and escaped to America. Wrote a number of
articles in America on Irish history and culture. Accompanied
remains of Terence Bellew McManus (the Irish/Liverpudlian
insurrectionist who died in San Francisco in 1860) to Ireland.

CHANDLER, RAYMOND THORNTON (1888-1959) Famous
crime novelist and playwright (his many books include "The Big
Sleep" 1939, "Farewell, My Lovely" 1940, "The High Window"
1942, "The Lady in the Lake" 1943). His mother was born in
Waterford of an Irish Protestant family, the Thorntons. His
maternal grand-father is believed to have been at one time the
principal solicitor in the law practice now known as Kenny,
Stevenson and Chapman.

CHEASTY, JAMES, (b. 1928) Playwright. Born Carrigavoe, Co.
Waterford . Left school at an early age to work on the family
farm. His first play , "A Stranger Came" was written in 1953
and produced that year at the Studio Theatre Club, Dublin.
Then came "Prisoners of Silence" which attracted much
admiration, and "Francey", which was first staged by the Smith
School of Acting, Waterford, and then at the Olympia Theatre,
Dublin. "The Lost Years" was also staged at the Studio Theatre
Club, Dublin, in 1957. He published a novel, "The Captive" in

1965. In 1968 "All set for Birmingham" was staged at the Theatre Club, Henrietta Street. In 1995, as part of its 60th Anniversary, Waterford Dramatic Society produced his latest play, "The Passing of Morgan Carey", directed by Jim Nolan.

CHERRY, WILLIAM and RICHARD. In 1802 the Cherry brothers began brewing in Peter Street and later (1806) opened an additional premises at King Street (O'Connell Street), eventually closing the brewery at Peter Street. In 1818 the partnership was dissolved and William took over the company. In 1828 Cherry's Ales bought the Creywell Brewery in New Ross and moved most of the business there. In 1952 the family sold out to Guinness. In 1955 Guiness bought the Davis Strangman Brewery in Waterford and commenced brewing "Cherry's No.1 Ale" there, thus completing the return to Waterford after 127 years.

CHRISTMAS, RICHARD, of Whitfield, Mayor of Waterford (1695 - 1696) encouraged traders of all descriptions and from all parts of the world to come to the city. Following this a number of merchants, Catholics, Protestants and Jews, came to Waterford from Italy, Spain, France , Portugal and Holland, and settled here. His successor, John Mason (1696-1698) continued this policy and, as a result "houses were repaired, ships built and trade began to flourish". In June 1701, a Jewish merchant, Jacob Nunes, applied to the Corporation for admission to the freedom of the city in order to trade, and received it in 1702. (ref. Louis Hyman)

CLANCY, LIAM. Singer and entertainer. Born in Carrick-on-Suir, Co. Tipperary. Educated locally. After leaving school, he worked in an insurance office while nursing ambitions to be an actor. A chance meeting with an executive of an American recording company (Tradition Records) gave him a job in New York. He had met Tommy Makem in Ireland beforehand and they had played music together. Now he was joined in New York by Tommy and Tom and Paddy Clancy. They began to play together and soon were eagerly sought after at folk venues in New York state. An early LP, recorded in 1959, "Come Drink a Glass with Us", found its way back to Ireland and by popular demand, The Clancy Brothers and Tommy Makem followed. By now they were well-known and had appeared on a number of TV shows including "The Ed Sullivan Show" which was re-broadcast around the world. In 1969 Tommy Makem went solo and the group disbanded. Liam moved to Helvick but still did gigs and made recordings with Tommy. He bought the well-known pub, "T. & H. Doolan's" in Waterford, and, for a few years, it was the centre of good folk music in the South-East. In 1974, he sold the pub and moved to Calgary, Alberta, where he hosted his own TV series on CBC. However, Helvick soon reclaimed him and he resettled there in the Eighties. His home there incorporates a state-of-the-art recording studio which he has used for making new recordings. In 1997, in conjunction with Donal Clancy and Robbie O'Connell he produced the LP: "Clancy O'Connell & Clancy ", and in the same year contributed three songs to the National Symphony-backed LP, "Who Fears to Speak of '98", issued to commemorate the 200th anniversary of the Rising of 1798.

CLEARY, WILLIAM J P (Bill) (b. 1926) Long distance walker and fund raiser. A member of a well-known family from Parnell Street, Waterford (his father was D. J. Cleary, a founder of Waterford Beagles). Educated at Waterpark College. In 1943, he changed his birth certificate to show his age as 18 instead of 17 and joined the RAF at Podgate training camp. He had applied to train as air-crew but found he was one of thousands in a waiting list and resigned himself to ground duties where he did "anything and everything". Returned to Ireland in 1948 but was unable to find work. Returning to Britain, he worked in Birmingham for a while before re-joining the RAF (in 1950), this time as air-crew. For the next ten years he flew as air-crew in Shackelton bombers as part of the Long-Range Maritime Reconnaissance Squadron. In 1953 he married Sarah Houldsworth, daughter of the racing driver John Russell Houldsworth, who was killed at Brooklands at the age of 22. From 1960 to 1965, he trained and worked as an RAF air traffic controller before becoming a teacher. During the 1960s he discovered a liking for long walks when, on a whim, and without any training, he took part in the Civil Service London to Brighton Walk. Several hundred walked the 53 miles. Bill

Cleary came 13th. In 1990, Bill and Sarah retired to Rathmoylan and in February 1993, again on a whim, Bill set out to walk to Mallin Head. In spite of some blisters and a very painful thumb injury, which necessitated an unplanned two-day stopover at Foulksrath Castle, Co. Kilkenny, the walk was completed in 16 days, after which Bill took out his pensioner's card and got the train home. In 1994, at the age of 68, Bill undertook a long and somewhat gruelling walk around Ireland in order to raise funds for the Royal National Lifeboat Institute, and went from Lifeboat Station to Lifeboat Station. In 62 days he walked 1,340 miles and collected over £7,000.

CLEGGETT, Charles (c. 1740-1820) Musician and inventor of musical instruments. Born in Waterford he became leader of the Smock Alley Theatre orchestra in Dublin. Moved to London and became "a favorite of Hayden". He died in London in 1820.

COAD, PADDY (1920-1992) International footballer, born in Waterford. Played for Waterford, then Shamrock Rovers (1941). Scored 126 League of Ireland Goals and was on the Shamrock Rovers team which gained three League Championships (1954, 1957, and 1959). Scored 41 FAI Cup goals and won 4 cup-winner's medals plus 11 international caps between 1947 and 1951. Later coached and managed Waterford and brought them to their first League title (1966).

COGHLAN, JEREMIAH In 1789 Jeremiah Coghlan inherited Ardoginna House on about 400 acres of land on the cliffs near Ardmore, from his brother Henry. Although the estate was modest, he and his wife were determined to make their mark in society and spent much of their income in adding castellations and turrets to their rambling house. They had three daughters, renowned for their beauty, and all three were popular guests at social occasions in Youghal. The fact that they always seemed to be dressed in the finest of silk resulted in a rumour (quite possibly true), that their father was a smuggler. They all made 'good' marriages. The eldest, Anne, married Lord Barrymore, Earl of Cork and friend of the Prince Regent. Elizabeth married the French Count de Castries, in exile in London, and the third girl became the wealthy Countess Llandaff. Ardoginna House eventually passed to the Count de Castries' grandson, Marshal Macmahon, who, having suppressed the Paris Revolution of 1870, was elected President of France.

COGHLAN, Captain WILLIAM CHARLES (1829-1916) When Sir Horace Plunkett, the great founder of the agricultural co-operative movement in Ireland, began his campaign in 1890 with the slogan, "Better Farming, Better Business, Better Living", one of his ardent supporters was Captain William Coghlan of Dromina, Woodstown, Co. Waterford, a retired army officer and JP. In the face of determined opposition from agricultural merchants, Captain Coghlan encouraged Plunkett's agent, R. A. Anderson, to hold discussions with farmers in the Gaultier area which resulted, in 1894, in the founding of Gaultier Co-Operative Society, one of the first co-ops in the South-East of Ireland.   Coghlan was elected chairman, a position he held for twenty years. During this time he continued to seek improvements in the marketing of farm produce and was an early advocate of selling all livestock by weight.   In 1863 he married Mary Kate Smithwick of Kilkenny.   The other members of the first board of management of Gaultier Co-Op were; Martin O'Brien, Brownstown; John Fitzgerald, Rathmoylan; John McCarthy, Credan; Edmund Phelan, Ballyglan; Patrick Murphy, Leperstown; F.G. Kent, Island View; Henry Morris, Belle Lake; and James Phelan, Dunmore East.   Captain Coghlan was also on the panel of magistrates for the Gaultier area and along with other magistrates sat at the Petty Sessions in Callaghane. In 1900, he was appointed to the Council of Agriculture by the new Department of Agriculture for Ireland headed by Horace Plunkett. Captain Coghlan's family continued to be represented on the board of management of Gaultier Co-op up to 1998 in the person of his grandson, Kevin Coghlan.

COLLINS, EDDIE (b.1941) Politician. born in Waterford and educated at Mount Sion, Waterpark College and UCD. Member of Waterford Corporation 1964 to 1981 and of Waterford County Council 1979 to 1981. Mayor of Waterford 1975-76. Ran for Dáil Éireann unsuccessfully in 1966 at the age of 25. First elected to the Dáil for Fine Gael in 1969 and at every election since then up to 1982. He was frontbench spokesman on Education from

1971 to 1973 and from 1977 to 1981. He expected to be appointed Minister for Education in the new government of 1981 and was bitterly disappointed when given a junior ministry in an offhand way at, and in front of, a hurried gathering of Ministerial appointees. He turned down the first offer of Junior Foreign Affairs minister, and swapped it with Jim O'Keefe for the junior ministry at Industry, Commerce and Energy. However, he resigned from this post not long afterwards, following allegations from socialist members of the coalition that a conflict of interest might exist between his junior cabinet post and his family firm. He failed to regain his seat in the next election.

COLLINS, JOHN (1883-1954) Public servant. Born in Waterford and educated at Mount Sion CBS. Joined Civil Service in 1902 and worked in different posts until 1948 when he retired as Secretary of the Department of Local Government. During the Second World War he was regional commissioner for counties Kildare, Dublin, and Wicklow, charged with the task of operating the machinery of government in the event of an invasion. He also acted as commissioner in counties Roscommon and Kerry following abolition of the county councils there, and as commissioner for the Fever Hospital, Cork Street, Dublin. In retirement, his expertise was called upon to revise local government law. His book, "Local Government", published posthumously, was regarded as the definitive work on the subject.

COMERFORD, PATRICK (d. 1652) Born in Waterford. Became a member of the Augustinian Eremites. Nominated bishop of Waterford in 1629 and consecrated at Rome. A supporter of Father Luke Wadding and Papal Nuncio Rinuccini. Died in France, buried in the Cathedral of Nantes.

CONGREVE, JOHN. Of Mount Congreve, County Waterford. High Sheriff of County Waterford, 1755. In 1758 he married Mary Ussher, daughter of Beverley Ussher, of Kilmeaden. His eldest son, John, lived at Landscape, near Kilsheelan but died without issue. His second son Ambrose, was the great-great-grandfather of the present owner of Mount Congreve, also

Ambrose Congreve, who was born in 1907, and educated at Eton and Cambridge before serving in the British Army during the Second World War. The Congreves were a merchant family with interests in shipbuilding and had a dry-dock facility on the river Suir near Newtown in the eighteenth century. In 1870 another Ambrose Congreve was Deputy Lieutenant of the county and a Justice of the Peace. The present Ambrose Congreve has spent much of his long life building an enormous collection of ornamental and flowering shrubs and trees. The garden, at Mount Congreve, Kilmeaden is truly unique and one of the most impressive, not only in this country, but in Europe. Protected by longstanding beech and oak woods on the banks of a broad stretch of the river Suir, the gardens extend to 110 acres and contain, according to Marianne Heron, "over 3,000 varieties of rhododendron, 600 types of camellia, 300 varieties of magnolia and 250 types of Japanese maple". Ambrose Congreve has set up a trust which will ensure that this beautiful place is left to the nation complete with funding for its maintenance for 25 years.

CONNOLLY, MAURICE (b. 1938) Playwright. Born at Cullinagh, Kilmeaden on March 25th 1938. Attended De La Salle College, Waterford. Worked for some time in London. In 1965 his first play "Ebbtide" was premiered in the Theatre Royal, Waterford. It was very successful and "packed theatres wherever it played" (Michael Browne). In 1966 he wrote "Weekend Appointment", another success and a Festival Award winner. In 1995 he wrote "The Magic Maker". He spent some years as a publican and an auctioner . He is married with two sons and farms at Dunanore, Foulksmills, Co. Wexford.

CONNOLLY, SYBIL (1925-1998) Fashion designer. Born in Wales, Educated at the Convent of Mercy, Waterford. Studied dress designing in London before returning to Dublin to work in the Richard Alan shop. In 1950 she established her own couturier business and became internationally well-known in a very few years. One of her most famous clients was Jacqueline Kennedy during the latter's time as America's First Lady. Sybil Connolly was also a Cordon Bleu cook and an expert on Georgian architecture, and towards the end of her life realised an ambition to write. In 1984 she published "In an Irish House", and in 1986 she co-edited "In an Irish Garden" with Helen Dillon.

CONNORS, FRANCIS (b. 1962) International Showjumper. Born at Pallas Stud, Woodstown, Co. Waterford. Eldest son of Mick Connors, the well known exporter of horses and former master of the Woodstown Harriers.   Educated at Waterpark College, 1966 -1979. Worked for his father for ten years as a showjumper and showed great natural talent.   Established his own stable in 1989. Apart from being constantly in the top three places in showjumping around the country, he is one of Ireland's most important riders on an international level.   Was Leading Showjumper of the Year, 1991-1995, and again in 1997. He was National Showjumping Champion in1993.   He has represented Ireland on the Aga Khan team at the RDS on several occasions. On "Diamond Express", he won the Hickstead Speed Darby three times.   His own favourite achievement was winning the Canna Cup on "Spring Elegance" at the Calgary-Du Maurier International Show in 1995. This is probably the biggest showjumping event in the world, with a huge international entry.   In 1997 he made a valiant attempt to break the Bareback High Jump record which stood at 7 feet, but had to retire after reaching 6 feet 11 and 3/4 inches! In 1988 he married Helen Walsh of Carrick-on-suir. They live at Ballylawn Stud, Kill, Co. Waterford.

COOKE, HESTER (d. 1988) Poet. Daughter of Canon Alfred H. Cooke, formerly rector at Carrick-on-Suir. She was devoted to her father, and when her mother died she stayed with him until he died in 1958. She wrote simple but evocative verse about the countryside and in particular, her native Waterford.   She published three small volumes of poetry. A popular poem describes Portally, near Dunmore East :

> "A small grey cove where white-edged waves are breaking,
> The call of sea birds circling around the bay,
> Tall cliffs where heather whispers in the breeze,
> And sea-pinks grow between in bright array.

A place your heart must always brim with gladness,
For everything around so happy seems,
The kind of place where oft you've longed to wander,
And only hoped to find in dreams.

Oh, tired feet a-tramping city pavements,
Ah, weary hearts that find no rest each day,
Could you but know the peace and splendour,
Abiding now around Portally Bay."

COX, LEMUEL (fl.1793/94) Was a professional bridgebuilder from Sheepscott, near Boston, (U.S.A.), hired by a Waterford company specially established by Act of Parliament to build a bridge over the River Suir. He had already built bridges over the River Foyle in Derry, and at Portumna. A total of £30,000 pounds was subscribed by the shareholders led by chairman Sir John Newport, which was to be re-paid with interest by tolls collected on the bridge. Work commenced on April 30th 1793 and the bridge, which was built of American oak, was completed on January 18th 1794 at a total cost of between £13,000 and £14,000. Lemuel Cox was granted the Freedom of the City for his work. Not only was he well within the budget, but his wooden bridge, which became known to several generations of Waterfordians as "Old Timbertoes", lasted for 117 years, until it was replaced in 1911 by the Redmond Bridge, a reinforced concrete structure which lasted for only 80 years. "Old Timbertoes" turned out to be a good investment. In 1824 the tolls were in excess of £4500, and by that year the original shares had doubled in value. Eamonn McEneany states (1992) that in 1852 an offer for the toll-rights of £45,000 was refused.

CROTTY, WILLIAM (d. 1742) Highwayman. Believed by some to have been born at Churchtown, Co. Waterford, and by others to have been born in Russelstown near Clonmel (Patrick C. Power). Roamed the areas around the Nire Valley and the Comeragh Mountains, but also preyed on the rich of South Kilkenny. He had a hideout in a cave overlooking a small mountain lake in the Comeraghs now known as Crotty's Lake. He was betrayed by one of his men called Norris and eventually captured. Hanged at Waterford with his associates John and

William Cunningham in 1742. According to Canon Power, sometime after his execution his head was cast into a pond or boghole at Coolgower.

CROWLEY, CARRIE (b. 1964) Broadcaster and TV presenter. Born in Waterford. Educated at St John of God's School, Passage Road, the Ursuline Convent, and St Patrick's Training College, Dublin, where she trained as a teacher. Taught as a temporary teacher in the Mercy Convent School, Dunmore East, and at Ballybeg, Waterford. In the late Eighties, she formed, with Jane O'Brien-Moran and Emer Power, a close harmony singing group called "Miss Brown to you". In the early 1990s, she started working as a part-time broadcaster with Waterford's radio station, WLR-FM and soon became a popular full-time broadcaster and presenter. In 1996 she joined RTE TV on the children's programmes "Echo Island" and " The Morbegs". In 1997 she was choosen to present the Eurovision Song Contest on TV and won international acclaim for her smooth, sophisticated and charming presentation of this high-profile television event.

CULLEN, MARTIN (b. 1954) politician and goverment minister. Born in Waterford. Educated at Waterpark College, Waterford Regional Technical College, and the Marketing Institute of Ireland. Worked for Grants of Ireland and African Distillers, Rhodesia, 1973 - 1976; as estate agent with Palmer & Co; and as director of Waterford Properties Ltd., 1976-1981. Regional Manager, Edward Dillon & Co. 1981-87; Chief Executive, Federation of Transport Operators , 1989-1992. Elected to Dáil Éireann for the Progressive Democrats 1987-1989, and was a member of the Senate 1989-92. He was elected to the Dáil for the PDs again in 1992 but crossed the floor to the Fianna Fáil party at the invitation of Albert Reynolds in 1994. Re-elected to the Dail on the Fianna Fail ticket in 1997. Had hoped for a full Ministry in Bertie Ahern's coalition government with the PDs but had to be content with the junior ministry at the Department of Finance. While in this position he has ensured that significant funds promised during the election have to a large extent been delivered to organisations such as Waterford Institute of Technology. A member of Waterford Corporation , 1991-1997, and mayor of Waterford, 1993-94. Lives at Abbey

House, Ferrybank, Waterford.

CUMMINS, MAURICE E. (b.1953) politician, mayor of
Waterford. Born May 25th 1953, son of John and Margaret (nee
Hennessy) Cummins. Educated at Portmarnock N.S., St
Joseph's CBS, Fairview, (1951-57) and the Irish Nautical College
(1960 - 62). Joined Irish Shipping as a cadet and later served at
sea with other companies rising to the rank of Captain. Joined
Bell Lines and over a period of some years rose to the position of
shipping terminal manager. In 1992 he joined Euro-link. He has
served as president of the Irish Chamber of Shipping, president
of the Waterford Chamber of Commerce (1990-1991 and 1994-
1995) and mayor of Waterford 1995-1996.

CUNNINGHAM, PETER (b.1947) Author. Eldest son of Major
Redmond Cunningham, M.C., (q.v.) and Mory ("Nicky")
McIntyre. Educated at Waterpark College, Glenstal Abbey and
UCD (B.A.). Wrote articles and short stories throughout school
and college years. Became a fellow of the Irish Institute of
Chartered Accountants (F.C.A.) and embarked on a business
career. In 1986 he wrote his first novel, ("Noble Lord"), and
began to move towards writing full time. Over the next five
years, he published a book each year, all of them thrillers: "Noble
Lord" (1986), "All Risks Mortality" (1987), "The Snow Bees",
(1988), "The Bears Requiem" (1989), and "Hostile Bid" (1990). In
1993 he published "Who Trespass Against Us", a quasi-thriller,
and moved from there to "Tapes of the River Delta" (1995), a
contemporary novel set against the recognisable background of
a south of Ireland port town. "Consequences of the Heart",
(1998) continued the theme. His novels are published in Britain
and the United States, and in translations. He writes a weekly
'Diary' column for the *Irish Independent* 'Weekend' supplement ,
and is a regular contributor to the *Independent-on-Sunday*
'Review', The *Observer*, *Time Out*, and other newspapers and
magazines. In 1973 he married Carol Powell. They have had 6
children - Peter (who died in 1990), Joanna, Mory, Jessica,
William and Benjamin. They live in County Kildare.

CUNNINGHAM, REDMOND CHRISTOPHER (b.1916) Born
in Waterford, the 9th child of Bryan Cunningham, an alderman

and mayor of Waterford (and one-time election agent of John Redmond (q.v.), M.P. for Waterford), and Elizabeth ("Pigeon") Bowe. Following school in Waterford, he became apprenticed to local architects, but shortly after the outbreak of World War II , joined the British Army where he was gazetted as a second lieutenant in the 79th Armoured Division. On the morning of D-Day, Captain Cunningham's troop landed at Ouistreham on the coast of Normandy and made significant gaps in the German defences. For this action he was awarded the Military Cross, the only Irishman so decorated on D-Day.   During the campaign through France, he was awarded the Croix de Guerre.   By February 1945, he was in the Rhineland, and was once again mentioned in despatches when he led operations resulting in the capture of 200 German prisoners. Another Military Cross was awarded. He de-mobilised in 1947 with the rank of major and returned to Waterford, having qualified as an architect.   In partnership with his brother, William (an engineer), he carried on a distinguished practice in the city for many years. He was a founder member of the company which built and ran the Tower Hotel and a number of other industrial enterprises.   His principle hobby was horse racing and he enjoyed a number of successes, notably the back-to-back victories of "Ross Sea" in the 1963 and 1964 Galway Plates.   He married Mory ("Nicky") McIntyre in 1946. They had five children: Peter, Rhoda, Pigeon, Redmond Daniel and Patricia. He retired in 1987 and moved to Dublin where he now lives.

D

DARGAN, WILLIAM (1799-1867) Railway contractor, born in Carlow, the son of a tenant farmer. Trained as a builder and surveyor under Telford in England. Returned to Ireland and began building Railways including the Waterford-Tramore Line. Became very wealthy and financed many other businesses, not always wisely. Organised and financed the Dublin Exhibition of 1853 at enormous expense to himself. Offered a baronetage but gracefully declined the honour. The National Gallery was built to commemorate him, and his statue stands on the lawn outside it.

DAWNAY, Major HUGH (b. 1932)   International Polo player and instructor. Born in India. Major Dawnay's father (General Sir David Dawnay) was a seven goal polo player who captained the British Olympic Team in 1936. After the Second World War Sir David was in charge of Ascot Race Course from 1952 to 1969. Hugh Dawnay's grandmother bought Whitfield Court, Whitfield, Waterford (built in 1840), from the Christmas family in 1916. Hugh Dawnay has himself captained the British Army Polo Team, representing the Army in many countries throughout the world, and has played for Ireland. In the nineteen-eighties, Major Dawnay opened the Whitfield Court International Polo School, the only one of its kind in the country, North or South. His book, "Polo Vision", is a standard textbook for the sport, and he travels the world giving instruction. He is well-known in the United States, where for twelve years he conducted an annual clinic at the Palm Beach Polo and Country Club. He has visited 30 countries to lecture and give instruction on polo. Currently he holds an annual clinic in Costa Careyes in Mexico. He is a founder member of the Waterford Polo Club, which trains and plays at Whitfield Court throughout the summer season.

DEASY, AUSTIN, TD (b.1936) Politician. Educated at CBS, Dungarvan and UCC (B.Sc., H.Dip. in Ed.) After graduation, worked as a school teacher. He was elected to Waterford County Council and Dungarvan Urban District Council in 1967. Unsuccessfully contested the General Elections of 1969 and 1973, and in the latter year failed to be elected to the Senate but was later nominated to the upper house by the Taoiseach. He was elected to the Dáil representing Fine Gael in 1977. Was frontbench spokesman on Fisheries from 1977 to 1979, and spokesman on Transport from 1979 to 1981. He was appointed Minister for Agriculture 1982 - 1987, and since then has been FG spokesman on Agriculture, Tourism and Transport, and Foreign Affairs. Last elected to the Dail in 1997 with a very comfortable majority, he has a high reputation as a public representative and is extremely popular in his constituency. His straight-talking, plain-speaking attitude to his work has earned him the deep respect of his political colleagues.

DE BROMHEAD, HARRY (b. 1936) Racehorse trainer. Born at Ardkeen, Waterford, the eldest son of John de Bromhead. Educated at Waterpark, Glenstal and UCD (B. AgSc.). Worked in the old family firm of Henry Downes Ltd. for a number of years while pursuing his passion for horses as an amateur jockey. He rode 33 winners during this time. In 1979, he handed over the reins of the family firm to his brother, Johnny, and became a full-time racehorse trainer and farmer at Knockeen, Co. Waterford. Has trained well over 350 winners including Thyestes Chase, Gowran Park, 1992; Grand Habit, Gold Card Hurdle, Cheltenham 1992; Fissure Seal, Heineken Gold Cup, Punchestown 1993. Another notable win was with "Bishop's Hall" (owned by Tom Carroll) in the Kerry Grand National (prize-money, £50,000) in 1996.

DE BROMHEAD, JEROME (b. 1945) Composer. Born at Ardkeen, Waterford on December 2nd, 1945. Educated at Waterpark, Killashee, Glenstal, Trinity College, Dublin (MA), and the Royal Irish Academy of Music. Studied with A. J. Potter, James Wilson, Seoirse Bodley and Franco Donatoni. He has written symphonic, vocal and chamber music which has been extensively performed and broadcast in Ireland and abroad. His 'Abstract Variations' (1976) which won First Prize at the Feis Ceoil Composers' Competition of 1976, premiered in

Dublin in June 1979 with the RTE Symphony Orchestra conducted by Albert Rosen. His Symphony No. 1 (1985), premiered on Jan 4th 1986, at the National Concert Hall, Dublin, with the RTE Symphony Orchestra conducted by Bryden Thomson. Amongst many other works, some commissioned by well-known musicians, was 'Concerto for Guitar and Strings', commissioned by John Feely and the Irish Chamber Orchestra with funds provided by the Arts Council, which had its premiére in March 1996 in the University of Limerick Concert Hall. He was elected to membership of Aosdana in 1986. In 1996, ill-health due to injuries received in a traffic accident forced his retirement from RTE Radio where he worked as a music producer. He lives with his wife and three sons in Killiney, Co. Dublin.

DE BROMHEAD, JOHN H. (1901-1988) Whiskey blender, farmer, amateur jockey and master of foxhounds. Father of Harry, Johnny and Jerome. Lived at Ardkeen, Waterford, on an estate now occupied by Waterford Regional Hospital. As a young man he was regarded as the best amateur jockey in Ireland. From 1930 to 1945, he was master and huntsman of the Gaultier Hounds. He spent many years as managing director of the family firm of Henry Downes & Co., wine and spirit merchants, where his skill as a blender produced a popular brand of whiskey, "Downes No. 9", although he himself was inclined to be abstemious, apart from two whiskeys each night before going to bed. The long-established premises of Henry Downes & Co. at Thomas Street had a number of huge casks on its flagged floors containing blends of whiskey. Cask No. 9 stood near the door and was used to serve customers who called in for a naggin of whiskey. Eventually, the customers themselves would call for "a naggin of No. 9", and this became the brand name for the Downes blend of whiskey.

DECLAN, Saint, (St. Deaglan) Traditionally believed to have preceeded St. Patrick, St Declan founded a monastery at Ardmore in the 5th/6th century, the 12th century round tower of which (99 feet) is still in excellent condition, alongside the ruined oratory (said to contain the tomb of St Declan) and cathedral.

DE COURCY, ERIC. Cellist, music teacher and president of Waterford Music Club. He taught music at Newtown School from 1945 to 1984. A founder member of the Symphony Club of Waterford.

DEEGAN, GERARD. (b. 1955) Champion Athlete. Born at John's Park on June 14th 1955. Educated at St Declan's, De La Salle College and W.R.T.C. Began running at the age of 11 with the De La Salle Athletic Club under the guidance of Brother Athanasius and later Donal O'Keefe. His first success was third place in the under-16 Cross-Country National Championships. At this time, he was also playing soccer with Bohemians and Gaelic football with Erin's Own. At the age of 17, while at the World Cross-Country Championships in Ghent, he chanced to meet American Collegiate Champion Neil Cusack (from Limerick), and as a result of a long conversation with him, decided to concentrate on running. Later that year, he won the under-18 Cross-Country National Championship. A year later, he won the under-20 National Championship. There followed no less than 4 (senior) National Championships in a row. He then skipped a year to go to the USA , and returned to win his fifth National Cross-Country title. He was also a member of the Waterford team which won six inter-county national titles; a record he thinks will be hard to beat because of the talent on the team which included Tom Ryan, John and Ray Treacy, Tom Aspel, Tom Jordan, Brendan Quinn and Roger Barron. From 1977 to 1978, he attended Providence College, Rhode Island, and won 3 championship medals and the bronze medal in the American National College Championships. He also won the gold medal for the 2-mile indoor race, and the silver medal in the 5000 metres track race. He represented Ireland 9 times in world cross-country races, only one less than the record of 10 held by his friend Neil Cusack. He has always had great respect for other runners and one of his fondest memories is of the 1978 World Cross-Country Championship in which he himself came 14th but the gold medal was won by John Treacy. Gerard Deegan now works with his father and brother in the well-known firm of Deegan Engineering of Poleberry, and lives in Waterford with his wife Colette, and their three children, Ami, Holly and Adam.

DEEVY, TERESA, (1894-1963) Playwright. Born at her family home, "Landscape", Passage Road, Waterford, she was educated at the Ursuline convent and, in 1912, entered UCD to study for a B.A. In 1914 her growing deafness caused her to transfer to UCC, and prevented her from taking a degree. She then wrote articles and stories and joined the Cumann na mBan, her interest in nationalism being fostered by her uncle Thomas, a priest and Land League activist. Her play, "Reapers" was accepted by the Abbey Theatre in 1930. Other successful plays were: "A Disciple" (1931), "Temporal Powers" (1932) "The King of Spain's Daughter" (1935), "Katie Roche"(1935), and "The Wilde Goose" (1936). After 1940, she wrote a number of original radio plays which were broadcast by Radio Eireann and by Northern Ireland Radio. A play on the life of Fr Luke Wadding, "Supreme Dominion", was highly successfull when broadcast by Radio Eireann in 1957. In later years, she wrote short stories, and a ballet, and co-wrote a children's book. She was elected to the Irish Academy of Letters in 1954. In the early nineties, the Abbey Theatre revived her most famous work, "Katie Roche". She died at Maypark and is buried in the family plot at Ballygunner.

DE HINDEBERG, RISTEÁRD (1863-1916) Irish scholar. Wrote "The Sounds of Munster Irish", 'being a contribution to the phonology of Desi-Irish; to serve as an introduction to the metrical system of Munster poetry' (1898).

DE LA POER, EDMOND ROBERT ARNOLD (1911-1995) 3rd Count de la Poer, de jure 20th Baron Le Power and Coroghmore, of Gurteen le Poer, Kilsheelan, Co. Waterford. Born on 25th February 1911, he was educated at The Oratory School, Edgebaston. On leaving school, he worked in the insurance business until 1936 when he was commissioned into the London Irish Rifles. In the 2nd World War, he served with this regiment and as a major with the Royal Ulster Rifles. In 1937, he married Rosemary Ann Miers who died in 1985. He subsequently married Geraldine Lanigan-O'Keefe who also pre-deceased him. Having succeeded to the title and the estate at Gurteen le Poer on the death of his father in 1939, the Count settled there after the war and over the years struggled to make the estate pay.

However, without training or natural ability in farming he found this a losing battle and in 1979, he sold the castle to the Rombelshein family from Germany, retaining the right to live there until he died. His one great passion was gliding, and he continued with this sport into old age. He was a founder member of the Clonmel Gliding Club. On his death, the title passed to his brother's eldest son, who works in the city of London. The original Barony of le Poer and Coroghmore was created by Henry VIII in 1535. On the death in 1704 of the Earl of Tyrone, the then holder of the title (as 8th baron), it passed to a kinsman, John Power. Unfortunately, John Power , who had been Mayor of Limerick, the last city to hold out on the side of James 11 against William of Orange, was made an outlaw, and went into exile with the Stuart king in France. The title was put into abeyance until 1863 when, by royal licence, the descendants of the "de jure" 17th Baron, John William Power, Liberal MP for the County of Waterford (1837 - 40), were granted the right to "henceforth use the surname of de la Poer in lieu of that of Power and bear the Arms of their original ancestors the de la Poers". In their appeal for this licence, the family had claimed that their ancestors had been companions of Strongbow. In 1864, Edmond James de Poher de la Poer, Lieutenant for the County and City of Waterford, and Privy Chamberlain to Pope Pius IX, was made a Papal Count.

DENN, PATRICK (d. 1828) Irish poet and teacher. Born at Upper Graigue in the parish of Modeligo, Co. Waterford, where his father Laurence, was a teacher. In 1824, Patrick Denn is recorded as operating a "stone, lime and thatched" schoolhouse in the Cappoquin area. It was a "pay" school and the annual fees were £6.00. In that year the school accomodated 49 boys and 11 girls. His poem, "Aighneas an Pheocaig" was published in Waterford in 1899. His manuscripts are preserved in St John's College, Waterford, and in the Royal Irish Academy, Dublin. There is a memorial to him in Cappoquin churchyard.

DOODY, MICHAEL (b. 1930) Waterford city manager. Born in Waterford and educated at Mount Sion Schools. Began working for Waterford Corporation in 1948. Studied accountancy and qualified as a Certified Accountant in 1963. Became City

Manager in 1972 and during the next twenty-four years, was very much involved in the process of change and evolution which brought Waterford from being a sleepy remnant of the 'old regime' to its present position as the vibrant, commercial (and possibly cultural) capital of the South-East. Amongst the great works which Doody supervised in this metamorphosis were the laying out of the East Waterford Water scheme, the replacement of the main drainage scheme of the city, the demolition of Redmond Bridge and the erection of Rice Bridge (1980), and the extension of the Borough Boundary (also in 1980) to encompass, in total, almost 10,000 acres , four times the area covered since 1898. Also, at the end of the Seventies, the city purchased land at Killowen from the Biddle family, and went on to establish Waterford Airport. Michael Doody gained most satisfaction, however, from the great strides made in urban re-newal, both in housing and commercial terms during his term as city manager. He retired in February 1996, and was given the Freedom of the City by Waterford Corporation.

DOONICAN, VAL (b.1927) Singer and entertainer. Born in Waterford city. Started playing professionally when he was twenty. Moved to London, and after a number of years "hit the big-time" with a chart-topper called "Walk Tall" in 1964. As he said himself, it took 17 years to become an overnight success. This was followed by two more hits ; "The Special Years" in 1965, and "What would I be" in 1966. He also had success with "My little Wooden Hut", "Scarlet Ribbons", "Little Green Apples" "Elusive Butterfly", "Morning", and "Danny Boy". He had a long-running Television programme on BBC where his easy-going, friendly , musical style and Waterford sense of humour made him popular with more than one generation. In 1997, at the age of seventy, he undertook a nine-day tour of Ireland, the highlight of which was a sellout show at the Forum (formerly the Regal Cinema), in Waterford.

DOWLING, DICK (1938-1998) Journalist. Born in Dublin of Waterford parents. His father was the late R. J. Dowling, political correspondent with RTE for many years. Dick started his journalistic career in 1954 at the age of 16 with the Waterford News. Four years later, Thomas Crosbie & Co. took over the Waterford News and amalgated it with the Waterford Star. Dick remained with the paper for the rest of his career, and became eastern correspondent for the other two papers in the Crosbie group, the Cork Examiner and the Evening Echo. He covered many stories of both local and national interest, including the mysterious and tragic crash of an Aer Lingus Viscount off Tuskar Rock in 1968 and the visit of President Kennedy to his ancestral home at Dunganstown, near New Ross. He also 'broke' the story of Jacqueline Kennedy's holiday at Woodstown. He had a particular interest in the sea and the fishing industry and was himself a keen drift-net salmon fisherman in his spare time. As a journalist, he had a reputation for honest reporting and insisted on verifying the facts of every story before sending it to the printing room. He suffered from heart disease in the last ten years of his life and died suddenly on January 3rd, 1998. His son Richard, carrying the tradition of journalism into the third generation, is a news correspondent with RTE.

DOWNEY, EDMUND (1856-1937) Editor and writer. Born in Waterford. Educated at the Catholic University School, Waterford. Worked in London for the publisher William Tinsley who published many leading novelists. Became an editor of Tinsley's Magazine. Returned to Waterford and became editor and proprietor of the Waterford News. Wrote and published a number of books including ; 'The Story of Waterford' (1914) 'A Guide to Tramore and it's Neighbourhood' (1919), 'The Glamour of Waterford', (1921), and, 'Waterford; an illustrated guide to the city by the Suir' (1924). He also wrote the novels. "Clashmore" and "Through Green Glasses".

DOBBYN. A name which has been associated with Waterford for over 300 years especially in legal circles. In 1752 Dr Richard Pococke refers to "Ballymakill (on the River Suir), the seat of Mr Dobbyn, a very ancient family". In 1788, no less than three Dobbyns were attorneys- at-law in the city: Andrew at Lady's Lane, Michael at Bailey's New Street and Arthur at Peter Street. In addition, Robert Dobbyn practised as a barrister at Lady Lane. When he died a diary was found in which he had made unflattering or scurrilous comments about most of his clients. In the same year (1788) a William Dobbyn traded as a carpenter, pewterer and hardware-man at Patrick Street. In the nineteenth century, Dobbyn and Tandy were solicitors to the Harbour Commissioners. In most of the 20th century, up to the present, Dobbyn & McCoy have been well-known solicitors, but there have been no partners of either name in the firm for many years.

DOYLE, GRACE (b.1977) Irish dancer. Daughter of Michael and Assumpta Doyle, Rockenham, Ferrybank, Waterford. A founder of Scoil Rince na Tri hAbhanna, she is the holder of Munster, All-Ireland, British and World Championship medals in Irish Dancing.

DUNNE, SEAN (1956-1995) poet and author. Born in Waterford, and lived for most of his early life at St Johns Park. Educated at Scoile Lorcáin, St John's Park, Waterford; Mount Sion CBS and UCC. Freelance writer and broadcaster who contributed regularly to Radio Eireann ('Sunday Miscellany' and 'Poetry Choice'). Published poetry: 'Against the Storm' (1985) 'The Sheltered Nest' (1982) 'Time and the Island' (1996) Edited The Cork Anthology (1993) and Poets of Munster: An Anthology (1985) and an edition of The Cork Review (1991). Published a moving biographical memoir of his childhood in Waterford entitled "In my Father's House" (1991) and a number of works of a spiritual nature including : 'The Road to Silence' (1994), and 'Something Understood : A Spiritual Anthology' (1995). He also wrote 'An Introduction to Irish Poetry' (1992) and was Literary Editor of the *Cork Examiner*. In 1997 an anthology of Irish Poetry, of which he had been the principle editor, was published by the Oxford University Press.

E

EDWARDS, FRANK (b.1907) Born in Belfast but raised at 102 Barrack Street. Educated at Waterpark College. Trained and qualified as a teacher at De La Salle College, and then took a teaching post at Mount Sion School. He was very much involved in the Republican movement (his brother Jack died in 1922 while a prisoner of the Free State troops) and had been a member of the IRA before joining the Republican Congress in 1934. In that year, he took leave of absence from Mount Sion to attend the Congress in Dublin against the wishes of his superior, Monsignor Byrne, who had been involved in negotiations with striking builders' labourers because of the effect the strike was having on work at Mount Sion School. The Republican Congress Committee in Waterford had many supporters amongst building workers and they in turn gave their full support to the strike. Frank Edwards had been warned by Monsignor Byrne not to attend the Congress meeting in Dublin on pain of loosing his job. However, the bishop of Waterford at the time, Dr Kinnane, decided he would be lenient, and instead asked Edwards to sign a document stating that he would have nothing further to do with the Congress. Edwards rejected this without hesitation. He was a popular teacher with many friends in sporting and political circles and gathered a lot of sympathy for his stand. He had been given three months to "recant", by the end of which he had a groundswell of support which included parents willing to withhold their children from school. The bishop then sent a pastoral letter to all the churches in which he said it "would be sinful to try to prevent the action of the manager (Monsignor Byrne) of the Christian Brothers School of Mount Sion from becoming effective", and went on to demand obedience to his authority "under pain of mortal sin". Seven hundred people showed up for a protest meeting in support of Edwards a few days later. Some pupils went on strike or picketed the school, there were scuffles between rival groups in the dispute, and the Gardai had to draw their batons on at least one occasion.

According to labour historian Emmet O'Connor, "The affront to Kinane's authority created a minor trauma in the city", which resulted in a number of bodies including Waterford Corporation and the dockers of the ATGWU issuing statements of support for the bishop, and undertaking to repel "the virus of Communism and Socialism". Edwards left Mount Sion, where he had been for seven years. He travelled to Spain and fought against Franco and fascism. He was wounded, and returned to Ireland. He was unable to get a job in any Catholic school, but was grateful to be given a teaching position in the Jewish School in Dublin. He later became secretary of the Communist Party of Ireland. He lived in Monkstown, where he died on June 7th 1983. (ref. Emmet O'Connor & Peter O'Connor)

EGAN, JOHN (d. 1888) Wholesale whisky merchant, tea and wine importer. Established a fine premises at Barronstrand Street, Waterford in 1854. Apart from a general trade in wines and spirits, Irish whiskey was exported to the United Kingdom and high-quality teas were imported from China, India and Ceylon. When he died in 1888, the firm was taken over by his sons, William and Edward, and in the 20th century by Edward's son, John, better known as Jack, who managed the business until his retirement in 1970. "Egans" was a very popular bar and coffee-house throughout the fifties and sixties, and remains a popular pub under the present ownership of Thomas Reid.

F

FARRELL, IAIN RIOCARD (b. 1938) Solicitor. Born Waterford, son of Riocard Farrell, (q.v.) Summerville House, Waterford. Educated at Waterpark, Glenstal Abbey, UCD and the Incorporated Law Society, Dublin (BCL, LLB). A partner in the well-known law firm of Nolan, Farrell & Goff since the early seventies. Waterford City Law Advisor since 1984; a position previously held by his father. Together, father and son have provided this service for seventy years. He has been Waterford Port Law Agent since 1962 and Spanish Vice Consul since 1975. Has spent a great deal of his life supporting and being involved in local or national organisations. Member of Waterford Rotary Club, Irish Georgian Society, An Taisce, Royal Cork Yacht Club, Fota Wildlife Park, etc. Founder and trustee of Waterford Maritime Museum 1978-80 (sadly now defunct due to lack of funding). Hereditary Freeman of Waterford City, Knight of Malta.

FARRELL, Capt. RICHARD J. (1898-1993) Ship's Master in Sail and Steam, Harbourmaster of Waterford. Born in Waterford on November 30th 1897, son of Richard Farrell, and uncle of R. J. Farrell (q.v.). Educated at Waterpark, and on leaving school at the age of 16, joined the White Star Line in Liverpool. Was given the position of deck boy on the S.S. *Medic* which carried emigrants to Australia. On the second voyage of this ship, in 1915, the vessel was taken to a naval dockyard in Australia and converted to a troopship. Australian infantry and cavalry (complete with horses) were loaded and transported to Alexandria for training. While there, the S.S. *Medic* took on the Munster Fusiliers and landed them at Sulva Bay, in the Dardanelles, under fierce bombardment. On returning to England, Richard Farrell joined the four-masted barque *"Jordanhill"*, as an able seaman bound for Australia, and returned to Le Havre via Cape Horn. In 1917 he served for 4 months on the barque *"Zayda"*, owned by Spencers of Waterford,

while studying for his 2nd mate's ticket. The *"Zayda"* carried
coal and the young Richard used to arrive back in Waterford
looking "as black as a pot". In the same year he began
attendance at the King Edward VII Nautical School in London
under Captain Maxwell of *Nicholl's Guide* fame, before joining
the 3-masted barque *"Killoran"* as 2nd Mate and sailing to
Australia and back to Dublin again by Cape Horn. In 1922 he
passed his final examination as Master in both sail and steam
(in 1992 he was the last surviving master in Ireland with a
ticket for sail and steam.) In 1927 he joined the S.S. *"Gogovale"*
as Chief Officer and travelled all over the world. In1931 he was
promoted to Captain of the *"Gogovale"* and continued in her
until 1940, when he applied for, and obtained, the position of
Harbourmaster at Waterford, where his uncle, Capt. Walter J.
Farrell (1862-1936), had been Harbourmaster before him.
Captain Richard Farrell was Harbourmaster at Waterford from
1940 to 1975, when he retired at the age of 78. He died on Jan
19th 1993, at the age of 95. He was a member of the
International Association of Cape Horners. He married, firstly,
in 1923, Frances Harbison, of west Limerick, who died in 1959,
and secondly, in 1963, Maeve Kenny of Stillorgan, Co. Dublin.

FARRELL, RIOCARD JOHN (1898-1984) City Law Adviser.
Born at Prospect House, Ardkeen, the eldest son of Austin A.
Farrell and Gertrude O'Mahony. Educated at Newtown School
and Bishop Foy School, after which he was apprenticed as a
solicitor to Henry D. Keane of O'Connell Street, Waterford.
Qualified as a solicitor in 1920 and shortly afterwards began a
practice at No. 33 George's Street. In 1929 he married
Josephine Britton of Fethard. They had a son Iain and a
daughter Valerie. Also in 1929, he was appointed Law Adviser
to Waterford Corporation, a position he held until his death in
1984. As a young man he was a Gaelic scholar. He spoke Irish,
played the bagpipes and often strode to Kings Inns wearing a
kilt, even during the Troubles. He was an accomplished tennis
player and a founder member, along with Olaf Deevy, Tom Heine
and others, of the St Anne's-Waterford Lawn Tennis Club.
Sailing was also a passion, and he was a founder member of
Waterford Harbour Sailing Club. During the last War he was
Officer in Charge of the local branch of the Maritime Inscription.

A Knight of Malta, he was also a hereditary freeman of Waterford, a right first conferred on his ancestor John Farrell in 1777. He remained active in his practice up to 1984, when he died, aged 86.

FEWER, MICHAEL (b. 1946) Author and architect. Born in Waterford, second son of Thomas (q.v.) and Mary Fewer of Gortmore, Newtown. Educated at Waterpark College and Bolton Street College of Technology (Dip. Arch., MRIAI) Lecturer in architecture at Bolton Street since 1979. Made FRIAI in 1997. A writer of books on walking in the countryside, and a regular contributor to *"Walking World Ireland"*. Publications include: 'The Wicklow Way: from Marley to Glenmalure' (1988), 'By Cliff and Shore: 'Walking the Waterford Coast' (1992), 'Irish Long Distance Walks'(1993) 'Irish Waterside Walks' (1997) and 'By Swerve of Shore' (1998).

FEWER, THOMAS MICHAEL (1910-1979) Company secretary and community leader. Born and raised at Newgate Street, Waterford. Education: Mount Sion CBS, Waterpark College, Institute of Chartered Secretaries, (AIIS, FIIS), and Irish Management Institute. On leaving school he joined Chambers & Halley as trainee accountant. Left before qualifying (1934) to join Allied Ironfoundries at Bilberry. Over a number of years became office manager and then company secretary, a post he held until he retired in 1973. In 1938 he married Mary (Maisie) Sheridan. He was actively involved throughout his life in local community, charitable and commercial activities. Joint Hon. Secretary, Waterford Boat Club, 1934-1937; officer in LDF, 1939-1946; Hon. Secretary, Waterpark Past Pupils Union, 1947-1948, and president 1951-1952; President of Waterford Chamber of Commerce, 1966-1968; member, Waterford Harbour Commissioners, 1968; founder member South-East branch, Irish Management Institute; founder member, Rotary Club of Waterford, member of the Committee of Management of Waterford City & County Infirmary; chairman, Waterford City Trader's Association, etc.. Although of a quiet and friendly disposition, he was fiercely proud of his native city and had a deep faith in its potential for advancement. In a speech to the annual dinner of Waterford Chamber of Commerce at the

Majestic Hotel in Tramore in 1968 he called for a second bridge for Waterford as "an immediate necessity".

FITZGERALD, ALEXIS (1916-1985) Senator, lawyer and government adviser. Born in Waterford on Sept. 4th 1916. Educated at Waterpark, Clongowes and UCD, where he studied Economics and Law. Qualified as solicitor, 1941, and began lecturing in economics at UCD. Founding partner of legal firm, McCann, White and Fitzgerald, in 1947. His father-in-law was John A. Costello, who, as Taoiseach, relied heavily on his advice in economic matters. Fitzgerald was a Fine Gael Senator from 1969 to 1981 and played a significant part in financial legislation. Taoiseach Garret Fitzgerald appointed him as a special adviser to the government in the Fine Gael-Labour coalition of 1981-82.

FITZGERALD, OLIVER (1910-1987) Physician. Born in Waterford, a brother of Alexis Fitzgerald (q.v.). Educated at Clongowes and UCD. Graduated B.Sc. (1933) and MB (1936) in first place with first class honours. Studied on a scholarship at Cambridge and Basle. As a consultant, continued to conduct important research in gastroenterology which provided an important basis for medical advances in this field. He was an editor of the *"Journal of the Irish Medical Association"*, first chairman of the National Drugs Advisory Board, and a member of the Medical Defence Union. He served a term as President of the British Society of Gastroenterology.

FITZGIBBON, JAMES J. (1920-1994) Champion tennis and badminton player. Born in Waterford and lived at Mayor's Walk. Educated at De La Salle College. As a tennis player he was capped 37 times for Ireland.

FLEMING, JOHN (1814-1896) Irish scholar. Born Ballyneil, Mothel, Co. Waterford. Educated at Kill village school. Schoolmaster at Carrickbeg and Rathgormack, 1849 to 1881. Due to ill health he took early retirement and cashed in his pension which soon led to extreme poverty. He was helped by the Royal Irish Academy and the Rev. Maxwell Close. Contributed to the *Gaelic Journal* and became its editor (unpaid). The articles contained in it provided much of the inspiration for the foundation of the Gaelic League. He contributed Irish Lessons to the National Teachers Journal (1872-1877) and published a life of Donnchadh Ruadh Mac Con Mara, (q.v.).

FLOOD, HENRY GRATTAN (1859-1928) Historian and muscian. Born in Lismore, Co. Waterford. Educated at Mount Melleray and the Catholic University (UCD) where he received a doctorate in music. In 1879 he became organist in Belfast, and in 1895 organist at the Cathedral, Enniscorthy. His "History of Irish Music" (1905) became a university textbook. He also published; "The Story of the Harp" (1905), "The Story of Bagpipes" (1911), "The Diocese of Ferns" (1916), "John Field of Dublin" (1920), "A History of Enniscorthy" (1920), and "Early Tudor Composers" (1925) He was made a Knight of St Gregory by the pope in 1922, and died in Enniscorthy in 1928.

FLYNN, PATRICK (b. 1956) Racehorse trainer, of Rathgormack, Co. Waterford. Educated at Rathgormack N. S. and at De La Salle College. Raised on the family farm where his father kept a mare or two and sent on the offspring for sale. In 1980 one of these, "Cheap Display" was returned from the sale and subsequently trained by Pat to give him his first win at Clonmel in 1981. The following year he had great success with "Virginia Deer" which won 4 races as a 2-year-old and went on to win 3 races at the Curragh before coming 5th at Royal Ascot. In the years since then his stables have become very well known and have produced about 300 winners. One of his personal favorites was "Montelado" which won the Trafalgar House Supreme Novice Hurdle in 1993.

FOLEY, DONAL (1922-1981) Journalist. Born in Ring, Co. Waterford. Educated at St Patrick's College, Waterford. Raised in Ferrybank, Waterford, and brought up as a fluent Irish speaker by his schoolteacher father. To-wards the end of the Second World War he emigrated to London and worked for the railways as a clerk. Joined the office staff of the Irish News Agency in London and soon found himself reporting on news stories. After the Agency closed he worked for *The Irish Press* and *The Irish Times* in London until he was called to Dublin by *The Irish Times* to take over the job of News Editor in 1963. He became Deputy Editor in 1977. In this role he gave particular encouragement to women journalists and was prepared to accomodate those with a radical viewpoint. He will be rembered mainly for his satirical column, "Man Bites Dog", and for his autobiography, "Three Villages", published in 1977.

FORTESCUE, HUGH, VISCOUNT EBRINGTON & EARL (1783-1861) The Fortescue family have connections with Ireland which go back to Elizabethan times, when a Royalist officer called Sir Faithful Fortescue received a grant of 2,000 acres in Antrim. Two members of what was to become the Fortescue family came to England with William the Conqueror, and fought by his side at the Battle of Hastings. It is said that one of them protected William with a strong shield and henceforth was christened Fortescue by King William. The family motto became "Forte Scutum Salus Ducum" (A strong shield is the salvation of generals). A Waterford connection began when Edmund Fortescue of London married (c.1650) Sarah Aland, eldest daughter of Henry Aland of Summerville (now Corballymore). At this time the lands attached to Summerville were substantial and extended almost to Dunmore East. Sarah died in 1668 and Henry Alland moved to Waterford where he became mayor in 1672-1673. The Fortescue family appear to have kept their interest in Summerville but the property was leased for most of the eighteenth century to Thomas Wyse.   There was no further word of the Fortescues until early in the nineteenth century when Hugh Fortescue took Summerville House and lands as a summer residence. He married Lady Susan Ryder in 1817, but she died in 1827 after only ten years of marriage. She was commemorated by the erection of an urn on an engraved plinth in the garden . The urn is long gone, but in a quiet corner of the now somewhat overgrown garden the plinth remains with the following engraving:

"To her whose hand traced these flowerbeds
during the last days of her residence here in November 1826,
Whose goodness cheered as her taste
adorned the surrounding scenes,

This urn is dedicated to record the grief
of her widowed husband
and the affectionate regrets
of her grateful neighbours"

She is also commemorated on a plaque on a former schoolhouse opened by her to provide schooling for the female children of the tenants. Hugh Fortescue was Lord Lieutenant of Ireland from 1839 to 1841, and in the latter year, on the death of his father, succeeded to the title of Viscount Ebrington and Earl Fortescue. The family appear to have been benevolent landlords and provided much employment in the area. Apart from providing schools they also contributed to the cost of building the local church. The Earl died in 1861 and was succeeded by his son Hugh, who by this time had made a career for himself as MP for Plymouth (1841-52) and as a Lord of the Treasury. The present house, in Scottish-baronial style, was built in 1878 by the 3rd Earl's younger brother, Dudley Francis Fortescue, although a section of the earlier house still remains. Dudley Fortescue was a Justice of the Peace and High Sheriff for Waterford in 1870. Early in the twentieth century the Fortescues sold much of the lands to their tenants under the new Land Act, and returned to England. The house was occupied for a time by a branch of the Gallwey family and others, before being purchased in the 1960s by Mrs Anne Klemn and her husband (who died within two years). Mr & Mrs Klemn went to great lengths to restore the beautiful woodwork of the house which had suffered from neglect and had been buried under numerous coats of paint by previous occupants.

FORTUNE, DESMOND (b. 1941)   Born and raised at Lower Newtown, Waterford. Educated at Waterpark College; Belvedere College, Dublin, and UCD, where he qualified as dental surgeon. He has always been a keen yatchsman and shortly after qualifying he undertook a sailing voyage around the Mediterranean. In 1970 he sailed his 37 foot yawl, *"Blue Peter"*, across the Atlantic via the Canary Islands, Antigua and Jamaica to Florida, experiencing many adventures on the way (a collision with a trawler and three weeks in the Doldrums when they ran short of water). After spending some time in the United States he sold his yacht and returned to Monkstown Co Dublin, where he began a successful dental practice which continues to this day. An active member of the Irish Dental Association, he was elected president in 1998. He continues to be a keen sailor, and in 1997 competed in the J24 European Championships in Plymouth.

FOSTER, ROBERT F. (Roy) (b. 1949) Historian. Born in Waterford, where his father was a teacher and lived at Summerville Avenue. Educated at Newtown School, Trinity College, Dublin, and in the USA. He has been Professor of Modern British History at Birkbeck College, University of London, and has held visiting Fellowships at St Anthony's College, Oxford, Princeton University and the Institute for Advanced Study, Princeton. Awarded British Academy Research Readership 1987-89. Elected a fellow of the British Academy, 1989. Currently is Carroll Professor of Irish History at Oxford. His many publications include; "Charles Stewart Parnell: The Man and His Family" (1976), "Lord Randolph Churchill: A Political Life" (1981) "Modern Ireland: 1600 - 1972" (1988) and "Paddy and Mr. Punch: Connections in Irish and English History" (1993). He was editor of "The Oxford Illustrated History of Ireland" (1989). An authorized biography of W.B. Yeats is due to be published soon.

FOY, NATHANIEL (1650-1707) Bishop of Waterford. Born at York, England. Educated at Trinity College, Dublin. Ordained in Church of Ireland. Canon of Kildare, 1670. Doctor of Divinity, 1684. Antagonised King James and spent some time in prison, but after King William's victory at the Battle of the Boyne he was appointed Bishop of Waterford and Lismore in 1691. On his death in 1707 he left substantial funds to the church and city for the establishment of the Blue School, for the "gratuitous education" of protestant children. A "handsome" schoolhouse was first erected at a corner of Baronstrand Street, but many years later (c.1808) it was re-established at Grantstown, Waterford. In more recent times, Bishop Foy School was established for a number of years in the Church of Ireland Bishop's Palace on the Mall, now the engineering department of Waterford Corporation. He died on December 31st 1707, and was buried in Christchurch Cathedral.

G

GALLAGHER, PATRICK (Paddy) (b. 1946) Newspaper editor and politician. Born in Waterford on December 18th 1946. Educated at Mount Sion CBS and the Central Technical Institute. Became an apprentice compositor at the Munster Express newspaper and over the next 18 years developed his skills in the printing business, becoming teletype operator and then proof-reader. He was elected as alderman to Waterford Corporation in 1974, and has been re-elected in every municipal election since then as a member of Democratic Left (usually close to, or at the top of the poll). In the January election of 1982 he was elected to the Dail, but lost the seat in the November election of the same year. Towards the end of the Eighties, he established, with John Morrissey and Joe Barry, the *"Waterford To-day"* newspaper, with offices in his front room. The first issue came out on September 28th1989, and was a tabloid-sized paper with 8 pages. The circulation in the early years was 10,000. Joe Barry subsequently dropped out of the paper, which is now a partnership between John Morrissey and Patrick Gallagher (who is also Editor). The paper now has 32 pages with an overall circulation of 20,600 and a circulation in the city of Waterford of 15,500 (certified by the Audit Bureau of Circulation).

GALLWEY, HUBERT D. (1915-1983) Genealogist and numismatist. Born at Woodlands, Half -Way House, Waterford, the son of Thomas Gallwey, K.M. His mother was one of the Powers of Faithlegge House. He was educated at Ampleforth and Christ Church, Oxford, and at the age of 22 was commissioned into the Royal Artillery. During the Second World War, in the battle for Crete, he was wounded and taken prisoner by the Germans, and spent the rest of the war in a prison camp in Germany. After the war, he stayed on in the British Army, but specialised in Education. He retired in 1959 with the rank of Lieutenant-Colonel and returned to Woodlands. His two great interests were genealogy and numismatics. He was editor of the

Irish Genealogist for 16 years and also wrote numerous articles for that publication and others. In 1970 he published "The Wall Family in Ireland, 1170 - 1970", a comprehensive volume based on intensive research which has been highly praised. In 1945 he was made a Fellow of the Royal Numismatic Society, and in 1962 he produced for the Society a catalogue of a large hoard of Roman coins from southern Spain, found in the main by himself while stationed in Gibraltar. He was greatly concerned about the environment, and was for some years chairman of the Waterford branch of An Taisce. On Sunday November 27th 1983, while entering the Cathedral in Waterford to hear 12 o'clock mass, he collapsed and died. (ref. Julian Walton)

GATCHELL, JONATHAN (1752-1811) Glassmaker. George and William Penrose founded the Waterford Glass Company in 1783 and in the same year employed Jonathan Gatchell as a junior clerk. John Hill, an experienced glassmaker from Stourbridge in England, was also employed and the two became good friends. In 1786 John Hill left Waterford Glass following a bitter row which was said to involve the wife of one of the Penroses. He had a secret recipe for making glass which he passed on to Jonathan Gatchell, who, on the strength of this valuable knowledge, was promoted to the post of senior compounder. Over the next thirteen years he continued to prosper until, in 1799, with two partners, he bought out the firm from the Penroses. By 1811, the year of his death, he was the sole owner and employed nearly 200 craftsmen.

GIBBON, E. A. of Rathculliheen, Waterford, was the founding chairman of Waterford Harbour Sailing Club. Several meetings were held in Dunmore East in August 1934 to establish the rules and aims of the club. The first committee consisted of E.A. Gibbon (chairman) Major Wilfred Lloyd, Harbour-master, R.T. Kelly, P.A. Anderson, Sir Ernest Goff, M. W. Gibbon, (secretary) and T. Colfer. The club had modest aims. Membership was to be confined to centreboard dinghies of 16 ft. or under, and the annual membership subscription was 5 shillings. The secretary then wrote to R. W. Morris and invited him to be Commodore. Mr. A. W. Anderson donated an "extremely beautiful" challenge cup to be raced for in Dunmore East each August.

GILLESPIE, FRANK (1929-1966) International jazz muscian. Born into a musical Waterford family (his mother was one of the Tuckers of John Street), he became one of Ireland's greatest alto-sax players. In 1960 the music paper "Melody Maker" published an article on the world's best modern musicians and listed Frank as 13th in the world in the alto-saxaphone category. He and Johnny Dankworth were the only Europeans mentioned. He played with many well-known bands, including Ted Heath and Joe Loss. (ref. M.Comerford & M. Dower)

GOODE, DECLAN (1914-1998) Hurler, footballer and GAA administrator. Born and raised in Dungarvan where he showed an early talent in hurling. At the age of 15 he was on the winning All-Ireland minor team (1929) and in 1931 a member of Waterford's first All-Ireland winning junior team. He was on the All-Ireland Senior Hurling team to reach the final in 1938 (where he excelled at full forward) though they were beaten by Dublin. He was a member of the winning senior county championship team in 1941. He became county secretary in 1938 and so began a period of great service (33 years) to the GAA which has rarely been equalled. When he died he was described by one writer in *The Waterford News & Star* as "a man who would go through fire and water in pursuit of a score", and "to generations of GAA folk in particular, he was someone very special." When he retired as county secretary in 1971 he was appointed honorary life president of the county board. He was an active member of the Fianna Fáil party and in 1967 he won seats on both Waterford County Council and Dungarvan Urban District Council. He remained a popular and active local representative until he decided to retire at the age of 80. He was elected chairman of Dungarvan Urban Council for several terms. He also served on the County Waterford Vocational Education Committee. He had a great love for Dungarvan and was buried in the old churchyard of St Mary's, just a few yards from his home.

GOFF, originally GOFFE. The Goff family came to Ireland in c. 1680, and originally settled in Horetown, Co. Wexford, on land given to them by Richard Cromwell. When Charles 11 was restored to the throne, this land was confiscated. However, when Richard Goffe swore allegiance to the Crown, they got their land back and lived on in Horetown until the middle of the 19th century, when they moved to Maypark House in Maypark Lane, and later built Glenville, a mansion in the Italianate style, also in Maypark Lane.

GOFF, Sir WILLIAM G. DAVIS, Bart (d.1917) of Glenville, Waterford. City alderman and a JP who was a great supporter of sporting organisations both nationally and in Waterford. These organisations included Waterford Boat Club (to which he presented the Goff Challenge Shield) and Waterford Bicycle Club. He was also the founding chairman of the Irish Automobile Club (which in 1918 became the Royal Irish Automobile Club) and in 1909 founding chairman of the Irish Aero Club. He had a passion for motorcars and was one of Ireland's first motorists, being the owner , in 1897, of a Beeston Motor Tricycle. He was the owner of the first car to be registered in Waterford city (a Napier, registration number WI -1). In 1903 he took part in Ireland's first hill-climb at Glendhue in the Dublin Mountains, winning his class in a Daimler car. In the same year a bill was introduced to allow the Gordon Bennett road race to be held in Ireland. The Treasury agreed to provide £1,000 pounds towards the cost of employing 2,700 men to assist in policing the 370 mile route through Carlow and Kildare. Sir William sponsored the Goff Cup for national motor trials. In 1905 he was involved in a fatal road accident in which a woman from Dublin died, but in a subsequent court case he was cleared of any blame. He was a director of the Waterford motor company of W. F. Peare Ltd, Ireland's first garage. Prior to his involvement with motorcars he had been an enthusiastic cyclist, and in 1895/96 he had erected at the People's Park a scientifically-designed and cambered cycle track (which replaced the ordinary track which had existed since 1880), and presented it to the Waterford Bicycle Club (founded in 1879). For several years it was one of the best cycling tracks in the British Isles and world class riders came to race on it. Goff was also active in the political and business affairs of the city. In 1892 he was appointed High Sheriff of County Waterford and in the same year elected vice-chairman of the Waterford, Dungarvan and Lismore Railway. In 1898 he was a director of the new brick factory at Bilberry. He had a life-long interest in technology and in 1904 was the Waterford representative on the national Board of Technical Instruction. As a Justice of the Peace he was a member of the panel of magistrates for Callaghane Petty Sessions. In 1900 his son, Capt. W. E. Goff was killed in action in Natal, South Africa. Sir William died in November 1917.

GOFF, ANNABEL DAVIS (b. 1939) Author. Born at Glenville, Maypark Lane, Waterford. Educated at Bishop Foy School. Has worked in television and films in London and Hollywood before moving to New York where she now lives. Published two novels: "Night Tennis" and "Tailspin" and a partial autobiography, "Walled Gardens: Scenes from an Anglo-Irish Childhood" (1990) which is a beautifully written account of her upbringing in Waterford.

GOODFELLOW, GEORGE (fl. 1959) Of English birth, George Goodfellow adopted Waterford as his home and opened a very popular shop, "The Sports Shop" on the Quay in the early 1950s. In 1959 he was one of the founding members of the Waterford International Festival of Light Opera. Tragically, while crossing the street to enter the Theatre Royal during the opening of the Festival in the early Sixties he was knocked down by a car and killed.

GOUGH, Sir HUBERT De La Poer (1870-1963) General. Born at Gurteen, Waterford. Member of a famous military family, his father (General Sir Charles Stanley Gough of Marlfield, Co Tipperary), his uncle (General Sir Hugh Henry Gough), and his brother (Brigadier-general Sir John Edmond Gough) all won Victoria Crosses on the field of battle (a record that has never been broken). His mother was Harriette De la Poer of Gurteen. He was educated at Eton and Sandhurst, comissioned as a cavalry officer, and served in India and in the Boer War. By 1914 he had reached the rank of brigadier and was serving at the Curragh Camp. He became the leader of the 'Curragh Mutiny', when officers stated that they would resign rather than lead troops in a show of force against the Ulster Volunteers who were threatening massive armed resistance to Home Rule. With World War One imminent, the British government side-stepped the issue and in the first year of the war Gough earned rapid promotion to lieutenant -general and the command of the 7th division and 1st Corps in France. He commanded the Fifth Army in the third Ypres campaign (1917), but was replaced by Sir Henry Rawlinson in 1918 following a successful German offensive at Mar.   Awarded KCB in 1916; KCVO, 1917; GCMG, 1919. He retired from the army as a full general in 1922. In 1931 he published his account of the 1918 campaign in "Fifth Army", and his role as commander of the Fifth Army was vindicated by Lloyd George in his "War Memoirs" (1936)   He was awarded the GCB in 1937, and commanded a London zone of the Home Guard from 1940 to 1942. Published his memoirs, "Soldiering On" in 1954. He died in London.

GOUGH, NEIL   (b. 1970)   Champion Boxer. Of Lisduggan, Waterford. A member of St Paul's Club, Lisduggan, Neil is six times National Senior Welterweight champion and has boxed for Ireland on numerous occasions.   In the World Boxing Championships of 1997 he narrowly missed winning a medal. Having had to fight 4 contests in a row, he won 3 but was defeated by 4 points in the final contest with Russian Olympic Gold Medalist, Oley Saitov.

GREATRAKES, VALENTINE (1629-1683) Also known as Greatorex. Faith healer, of Affane, Co. Waterford, who lived in Affane Castle (which he leased from the Boyle family) on the site of Affane House. Educated at Lismore. Served in Cromwellian army under the regicide Robert Phaire (or Phayre). Was rewarded with the offices of magistrate and Clerk of the Court in Co. Cork. Started curing scrofula (the "Kings Evil", which was thought to be cured only by the royal touch) and other diseases by the laying on of hands in 1662. In 1666 he travelled around England giving cures, notably at Ragley, Worcester and Lincoln's Inn. He would not accept any payment, telling his patients to praise God if they were cured. He extended his cure to include rheumatism and other diseases. He became famous and hundreds flocked to receive his cure. He claimed not to have received any payment for his "cures", but was accused of quackery by the Oxford biographer, David Lloyd (1625-1691) whom he answered with "Brief Account" (1666), about himself and his cures addressed to Robert Boyle, and with testimonials from Andrew Marvell, Bishop Wilkins, Benjamin Whichcote, provost of King's College, Cambridge, and fifty others. In the same year he returned to Ireland where he died on November 28th 1683.

GREENE, JOHN (fl. c.1780) A Waterford merchant who established the first salthouse in Waterford at William Street, and lived at Greenville, Kilmacow.

GREENE, PATRICK (Paddy) (1916-1997) Hurler and keen hurling supporter. Born in Waterford and lived most of his life at Mount Sion Avenue. A member of the Waterford panel for the 1938 All-Ireland match in which the county was defeated by Dublin, he was a founder member of Mount Sion GAA Club, which in the same year won the first of 4 senior club titles. In later life he was a trainer and selector and trained the club to seven county championships.

GRIFFIN, NOEL MARTIN (1926-1981) Managing Director of Waterford Glass. Born in Dublin on December 23rd 1926, eldest child of Joseph and Mairín Griffin. Educated at Newbridge College, Co. Kildare. Qualified as a chartered accountant in 1950. Boyhood friend of Jim McGrath, the son of the founder of the Irish Hospital Sweepstakes and the Irish Glass Bottle Co. chairman Joseph McGrath. Joined Waterford glass in 1950, where he became a director in 1952, and general manager in 1956. Made managing director in 1960. A director of the Irish Glass Bottle Co. Ltd since 1962, he was made group managing director of that company in 1964. In 1959 he married Ita Brennan of the well-known Galway family of that name. They had three sons and two daughters. For many years he was a high-profile representative of Waterford Glass and adopted an active and sometimes flamboyant lifestyle, very involved in racing, hunting and social occasions, and, in quieter times, shooting and fishing. He liked to discuss business over long lunches at the Tower Hotel, and his chauffer-driven Mercedes was almost a permanent fixture in the tour-bus parking slot. Yet he is said to have enjoyed the trust of, and a friendly and informal relationship with, the huge workforce at Waterford

Glass, and liked to walk the workshop floor to get down-to-earth opinions from his staff. Towards the end of his life he suffered from ill-health, and liked to spend his summer holidays in the peace and quiet of Dunmore East, swimming or sipping a beer on the slipway beside the sailing club. In August 1981 he went for a swim, got into difficulties, and drowned.

GRIMES, PHIL (1929-1989) One of Waterford's greatest hurlers. Born on May 8th 1929. A member of the Mount Sion Club, he began hurling at senior level in 1948 but halfway through the season went to the United States and thereby missed Waterford's first All-Ireland win. However, as a sub who had played in the championships, he was awarded a medal. He spent three years in the USA and played for Tipperary at Celtic Park, New York. He returned to Ireland and in 1957 was captain of the Waterford team which reached the All-Ireland only to be beaten by Killkenny. He was on the All-Ireland winning team of 1959 where he formed a magical partnership with Seamus Power at midfield, and was one of the highest scorers in the county. In 1963 he played fourteen games and scored 87 points. He won 4 Railway Cup Medals and captained Munster in their 1958 Railway Cup win. Apart from winning 14 Senior County Hurling Medals, he also won 5 Senior Football Medals. He died after a long illness on May 8th 1989.

H

HALE, ALFIE (b. 1939)   International Soccer player and football manager. Born in Waterford and educated at De La Salle College. As a teenager he played soccer with St Josephs Club. At age 16, he began playing at Waterford FC as an amateur. By 1957 he was a regular first-team player and had played for the amateur international team. In 1960 he was signed as a professional with Aston Villa and for the next 7 years he played in the English first division. In 1967 he re-joined Waterford F. C. and began what was to be one of the most successful careers in League of Ireland history, winning, over the next ten years or so, every honour in the game except a cup-winners medal. He has won 14 International Caps, 6 League Medals, 3 Cup runners-up medals, Shield medals, and Munster Cup medals. He has won 3 Player-of-the-Month Awards, 2 Munster Soccer Star Awards, many Sports Star of the Week awards, and the 1972/73 Football Personality of the Year Award. He was appointed Manager of the new Waterford United Football Club in 1982 and within a few years had sustantially improved the club's position. In 1984 the club reached the Cup semi-final. In 1984-85 the club won its first major trophy, the League Cup. In 1985/86 and 1986/87 the club won the Munster Senior Cup, and in 1986 reached the FAI Cup Final and so qualified for Europe. They came up against the mighty Bordeaux but acquitted themselves well. In the first match, at home, they lost 2-1. In the return match in Bordeaux , Waterford held this top team (they had 15 international players in the squad) at bay until 6 minutes before the end, when a flurry of activity by the French shattered the defence and   produced a winning score of 4 - nil. During his time as manager, Alfie Hale brought many top English clubs to Waterford, including Arsenal, Southhampton, Sunderland and Queen's Park Rangers. In 1992 his association with Waterford United came to an end.   He received the Merit Award of the Professional Footballers Association in 1994. In 1997 he was given the Soccer Writers of

Ireland Award for giving 40 years of service to Irish Soccer.

HALL, SAMUEL CARTER (1800-1889) Writer. Born 9th May 1800, at Geneva Barracks, near Passage, Co. Waterford. His father, Captain Robert Hall, an English soldier who had fought at Gibraltar, moved to southern Ireland in 1795 and invested most of his personal capital in copper mining. Unfortunately, the business failed and Mrs Hall had to move to Cork and set herself up as a milliner in order to support Samuel and his eleven brothers and sisters. At the age of 21 Samuel went to London and became employed as a journalist and editor of a number of small publications. During this time he met a young lady journalist ANNA MARIA FIELDING, who had been born in Anne Street, Dublin, in the same year as himself (1800). She was a lady of beauty and talent and the two were married on September 20th 1824. The two went on to become energetic writers and philanthropists, with probably Anna Maria as the main driving force. The Halls toured Ireland on several occasions. "Hall's Ireland" was first published in 1841 and was reprinted several times, each time with various additions or changes. The couple lived to a ripe old age. Anna Maria Hall died in January 1881 and Samuel Carter Hall in March 1889. They are buried in Addlestone Churchyard, Surrey.

HANSARD, JOSEPH (1835-1909) Printer, bookseller and historian. Born in Limerick but moved to Dungarvan, Co. Waterford, in 1860 having trained in the printing trade in Clonmel. By 1861 he was running his own business, and in 1862 married a local girl, Mary Jones. In 1870 he wrote, printed and published the work for which he is best known, "The History, Topography and Antiquities of Waterford City and County". Although, as the author himself states, based to a large degree on previous works by CHARLES SMITH (1746) and R.H. RYLAND (1824), this book is a useful addition to the literature available on the history of Waterford. Within a few years of its publication it had become much sought after and in recent times had become so rare as to fetch several hundred pounds per copy. This problem was rectified in 1997 when a new edition of the book was published by Waterford County Council under the editorship of the County librarian, Donal Brady. When

Hansard's wife died young, he re-married and moved to Killarney in about 1880, where he carried on the business of bookseller and printer until his death in 1909.

HARTLEY, FERGAL (b. 1972) The captain of the Ballygunner Senior Team which won all three of the County Finals for the years 1995, 1996, and 1997. He also won an Under-16 Munster divisional medal, under-21 Munster and All-Ireland medals in 1992, a Fitzgibbon Cup medal with Limerick University in 1994, and a Sargent Cup medal in 1989 and 1996. He was a member of the Waterford team which reached the final of the the National Hurling League (last won by Waterford in 1963) only to be defeated by Cork at Semple Stadium on May 17th 1998.

HARVEY, THOMAS NEWENHAM (1837-1901) Printer and businessman. Born at Cove Lodge, Waterford, the home of his grandfather, Thomas Waring. His father, a Quaker from Cork, established a stationery shop on the Quay. Thomas Harvey was educated at Newtown School and continued in the Quaker tradition. On leaving school he set up a printing business in Little George's Street. A contract with the Waterford & Limerick Railway for all their printing proved to be the stepping-stone to success, and within a few years the business was highly profitable. He was active in local charities and helped the Waterford Friends to raise £460 for the relief of Lancashire cotton workers laid off due to the American Civil War. He was secretary of the Waterford Society for the Prevention of Cruelty to Animals for many years up to 1897. Towards the end of his life he wrote his autobiography which was published after his death in 1901. He is buried in the Quaker graveyard at Lower Newtown.

HAYES, MICHAEL ANGELO, R.H.A. (1820-1877) Painter. Born in Waterford on July 25th 1820, the son of Edmund Hayes, a Tipperary artist whom he studied under. As a teenager he exhibited at the Royal Academy as "Master Hayes". He became a noted painter of sporting and military subjects and enjoyed drawing and painting horses at which he was especially skilled. He published a pamphlet " On the Pictorial Delineation of Animals in Rapid Motion"(1876) and was responsible for the

Bianconi "Car-Travelling" prints and many other engraved works (including the famous "Punchestown"). One of his best-known paintings (now in the National Gallery) is that of "Charles Brindley, (1817 - 1879), Riding to Hounds". He also illustrated the biography of Bianconi written by Bianconi's daughter, Mrs Mary Anne O'Connell. He served as Military Painter-in-Ordinary to the Lord Lieutenant and as Secretary of the Royal Hibernian Academy (1856). He was also secretary to the Lord Mayor of Dublin and City Marshall. He was involved in a libel action for caricaturing a former mayor. On December 31st 1877, he was accidentally drowned while examining a water tank at the top of his house, No. 4 Salem Street, Dublin.

HEARN, Rev. FRANCIS (1747-1801) Thought to have been born in Modeligo, Co. Waterford. Became rector of the Irish College in Louvain. He was an accomplished linguist and made great efforts to preserve the Flemish language. Often referred to as "the savior of the Flemish language" by the Flemings of Belgium, who had a public monument erected to him in Brussels. In 1799 he returned to Ireland and was appointed parish priest of St Patrick's, Waterford, by Bishop Hussey.

HEARNE, JOHN (1893-1968) Civil Servant and Lawyer, born in Waterford. Educated at Waterpark, NUI and King's Inns. Assistant parliamentary draftsman 1923-29. Legal Adviser to the Department of External Affairs 1929 - 1939. He is largely responsible for drawing up, at Eamonn De Valera's request in 1935, the principle heads of a new constitution for Ireland. He was High Commissioner to Canada in 1939 and Ambassador to the United States in 1950.

HEINE, THOMAS JOSEPH (b.1925) Watchmaker and jeweller, grandson of Andrew Heine, watchmaker, who came to Waterford from the Black Forest area of Bavaria in 1878 and opened a shop in Patrick Street. Thomas Heine's father, Alexander, married one of the Kents of Great Island, and Thomas married Nora Barry of Dungarvan. At the turn of the century the business moved to Barronstrand Street where it remains to-day with the fourth generation of the family involved in the business. Thomas Heine, who was educated at St Declan's and De La Salle

College, has been involved for most of his life in tennis and golf, and was one of the negotiators in the amalgamation of St Anne's and Waterford Lawn Tennis clubs. He was later elected president of the new club and remains an honorary life member. He is also an honorary life member of Waterford Golf Club.

HENCHY, CHRISSTINA (CHRISS) (b. 1932) Classical singer and musician. Born in Waterford, the youngest daughter of Thomas and Ellen (nee Shannon) Kelly. Was educated at the Presentation Convent and studied piano, initially with Bridie Cullinane of Mayor's Walk and later with Mary Timony. She sang on Radio Eireann at the early age of 18 and was paid 3 guineas, an enormous sum at the time. Her musical life was put on hold for a while when she met and married Reggie Henchy, and at the age of 23 she gave birth to her daughter and only child, Alison. She returned to her musical career under the guidance of Elizabeth Downey, whom she describes as her mentor and inspiration. Over the next few years she won a number of awards at the National Feis Cheoil, including 2 gold medals, the German Goverment Cup (for singing Bach) and the Charles Villiers Stanford Medal. The award of the German Goverment Cup brings back conflicting memories for her because on that day (the 17th of May 1974), she was standing in the doorway of the Metropolitan Hall in Lower Abbey Street, with the Cup in her hand, having just been photographed by the *Irish Times*, when a terrorist bomb went off a few streets away leaving many dead and wounded. At this time she was regarded by Willie Watt as "resident" contralto with the Waterford Music Club and was also involved with the Waterford Singers for eight years. She studied with the Royal Irish Academy of Music in Dublin, and under Dr Hans Valdemar Rosen, the founder of the RTE Singers. She won the Percy Whitehead Cup in 1974 for Lieder singing. She played a season at the Gate Theatre, Dublin, and with the Irish Theatre Company and Gemini Productions in Limerick. On the home scene she featured and starred in the first series of Tops of the Town and for many years afterwards. During the International Festival of Light Opera, partnered by Pascal Kennedy (a talented pianist) she provided a cabaret for the Festival Club. Although she divides her time now between her role as an examiner for the Royal Irish

Academy of Music and an organist at the Friary, Waterford, she is still in demand as a classical singer.

HENNESSY, CHRISTOPHER A. (b. 1940) Businessman. Born in Waterford, where his father was a well-known undertaker, he was educated at Mount Sion CBS before emigrating to England. There he became an apprentice mechanic in the motor business while studying at night at the London Polytechnic. He became a successful manager in the motor business, and in his spare time qualified as a private pilot and then as a flying instructor. He returned to Waterford where he established, with Dan Healy, the firm of H.&H. Motors, Waterside. He was also a founding member of Waterford Aero Club. In September 1980 he became the first Secretary and Manager of Waterford Airport. It opened in 1981 but did not become operational until 1983 when Avair operated a shortlived service between Cork, Waterford and Dublin. The first regular flight from Waterford to London took place on July 8th, 1985, by the newly formed Ryanair with a 15 seater twin-engined Banderainte aircraft. Chris Hennessy, faced with a very small budget, initially carried out almost all the airport responsibilities himself, always with efficiency and enthusiasm. Outgoing passengers would be greeted with a cheerful smile by Mr. Hennessy, who, having checked their tickets, would then put their baggage on the trolly for the plane. When baggage and passengers were all aboard, he would run upstairs to the little control tower and give the pilot permission to take off. He would then run downstairs and man the emergency fire tender (a jeep with two fire extinguishers). Nevertheless, this was the first daily, non-domestic flight outside the national Airports. Soon however, he had an air traffic controller and a real fire tender (Fifties vintage). In May 1986 Ryanair introduced a 44-seat HS748 and flew to Luton. Meanwhile, after much lobbying, Chris Hennessy had managed to get a licence to operate a duty - free shop, the first one to operate outside the National Airports, and it opened in July 1986. Other improvements took place under his management, including runway lighting with Precision Approach Path Indicator (PAPI) and an instrument approach procedure (aid to bad weather landings). In 1988 the pressure of running his own motor business and running an airport with limited resources became too great a burden and Chris Hennessy resigned as airport manager in March of that year. He continues to be an active member of Waterford Aero Club to which he donates his time as a flying instructor. He is Treasurer of Waterford Polo Club and is a full playing member. In the winter he hunts with the Waterford Hunt and the Kill and Woodstown Harriers.

HICKEY, JOHN (fl. 1990) of Lisnakill, Butlerstown, Co. Waterford, was a member of Waterford Adult Riding for the Disabled. He was a member of the Irish Team at the Special Olympics held at Strathclyde, Scotland in 1990, and was the winner of a Gold medal and a Silver Medal for dressage.

HILL, CHARMIAN (1918-1990) Born Charmian Dorcas Richards-Orpen. Married Dr. Parkinson Hill and lived firstly at Catherine Street , Waterford, and later at Belmont House, Kings Channel, Waterford. In later life was owner of the brilliant mare, "Dawn Run", which won the Champion Hurdle in 1984 and the Cheltenham Gold Cup in 1986, the first horse ever to complete this double. An almost fanatical horsewoman right into late middle age, Mrs Hill paid 5,800 guineas for a big three-year old filly by Deep Run. Only a year before she had had a serious fall at Thurles. Two years later, with the withdrawal of her permit by nervous authorities a strong possibility, she rode Dawn Run to her first win at Tralee in 1982 after overcoming stewards' doubts as to her fitness. After that it took a considerable effort to get this stubborn and determined lady in her sixties to hand over the reins to professional jockeys. In 1983 Dawn Run won her first race at Liverpool. In 1984 she won the Champion Hurdle and in 1986, by which time she had a huge Irish following, the Cheltenham Gold Cup. Richard Burridge (the owner of the famous grey gelding, Desert Orchid, which fell during the race), observed: "The hot favourite was Dawn Run, the pride of the Irish, and the Irish take Cheltenham very seriously.... There were incredible celebrations after Dawn Run's victory, and Charmian Hill, the mare's owner, was given the bumps in the winner's enclosure". Later that year, Mrs Hill entered Dawn Run in Auteuil near Paris. For some reason, she decided to change Dawn Run's jockey, and dismissed the mare's regular rider, Tony Mullins, in favour of the Frenchman Michel

Chirol. Most experts seem to agree that the sudden fall which killed Dawn Run was beyond the control of the jockey. The Horse & Hound's respected correspondent, John Oaksey, said; "As for the fall, the truth is that, throughout her career over hurdles , as well as fences, Dawn Run had never been a consistently accurate jumper. She has always been apt, without warning, to perpetrate sudden comprehensive blunders, – either standing off too far at hurdles, or, as at Liverpool, virtually ignoring a fence." Nevertheless, the death of Dawn Run is still a subject of controversy in Irish racing circles.

HOBSON, WILLIAM (1793-1842) Naval officer and colonial governor. Born in Waterford in 1793, he joined the Royal Navy and rose to the rank of captain. In 1839 he was sent by the British Government to formally take over New Zealand as a British colony, and became its first Governor General. He died in Auckland on September 10th 1842.

HOGAN, JOHN (1800-1858) Sculptor. Born in Tallow, Co. Waterford. According to Arthur Griffith he was "one of the five great sculptors of the nineteenth century; the Repeal Cap worn by O'Connell was modelled by him and Henry McManus, the painter, from the Irish crown" . This 'Repeal Cap' was placed on O'Connell's head by Hogan at Mullaghmast, Co. Clare, in 1843. Hogan was a devoted follower of O'Connell and was commissioned by the Repeal Association to sculpt the enormous marble statue of O'Connell (first unveiled in 1846) which still stands in the City Hall, Dublin. He also created the bronze statue of O'Connell erected in The Cresent, Limerick, in 1857. After starting his working life as a legal clerk in Cork city, Hogan became a carpenter at the age of 16, but when he revealed his talents as a draughtsman and carver he was encouraged by the architect, Sir Thomas Deane, to take up sculpture. For three years he attended Dr Woodroffe's lectures on anatomy. He received commissions from Sir Thomas Deane and Bishop Murphy of Cork. In 1823, William Paulet Carey, a famous art critic and dealer based in Dublin and London, saw his work and helped organise a public collection, supported by Lord de Tabley, the Dublin Society and others, to send him to Rome where he studied at the School of St Luke and the Vatican galleries (1824-48). Rome became his home, where he married an Italian lady and was accepted into the higher echelons of Roman artistic society, being elected (1837) to membership of the Virtuosi del Pantheon (founded in 1500). He made many trips to Ireland to undertake commissions and give his support to Daniel O'Connell. In 1848, revolutionary fever having spread to Rome, and an attempt at a Roman republic having been put down by the pope with the aid of French troops, Hogan returned to Ireland. There he worked for the next ten years and produced a number of important works including (in addition to those of O'Connell) statues of Father Matthew in Cork; Thomas Drummond in the City Hall Dublin; Dr Doyle the Bishop of Kildare in the Catholic Cathedral, Carlow; John Brinkly, Bishop of Cloyne in Trinity College; the "Dead Christ" in Clarendon Street Church ,"Eve", and the "Drunken Faun" in UCD. He died at his home in Wenthworth Place, Dublin on the 27th March, 1858.

HUMPHRIES, CARMEL FRANCES (1909-1986) Zoologist. Born in Waterford and educated at the Ursuline Convent, Waterford; Loretto Convent, St. Stephen's Green,Dublin; and UCD. Did postgraduate research in England and Germany (1934-1938). Assistantships in zoology at UCD and Queens University, Belfast from 1938. Lecturer in zoology UCD 1948 and professor 1956. Member of the Irish Committee of Science and its Industrial Application; Member, Institute of Biology. Irish representative of the International Limnological Association and the Freshwater Association, England.

HUSSEY, THOMAS (1741 - 1803) Roman Catholic bishop of Waterford and Lismore. Born in Co. Meath. Sent to study at the Irish College in Salamanca, Spain. Entered the La Trappe monastery. On orders from the Vatican he left the monastery, was ordained and became chaplain to the Spanish Embassy in London (1767). Met intellectuals such as Dr Johnson and Edmund Burke and was elected a Fellow of the Royal Society in 1792. When Spain joined with France on the side of the American colonists the Spanish Ambassador returned to Spain but Hussey stayed on and then, at the request of George III travelled to Madrid to try and persuade Spain to leave the alliance. His efforts failed, but he was recognised as a skillful diplomat, and in 1794 was sent to Ireland to investigate unrest amongst Catholics in the English army there. One of the problems was that Catholic soldiers were forced to attend Protestant services. When Private Hyland of the Irish Light Dragoons received 200 lashes at Carrick-on-Suir for refusing to attend a service on the advice of his priest, Hussey protested to London but was paid scant attention. He found himself pleading with soldiers to be patient, while seeing the groundswell of frustrated anger which might lead to real violence. On the other hand, the Castle resented Hussey's attitude and reduced communications with him. In a pastoral letter he referred to "the remnants of old repression" exerting their influence. His letter was greeted with anger by the authorities, and, ultimately, disregard. He helped to establish the Catholic Seminary at Maynooth and became it's first president in 1795. In 1797 he was made Bishop of Waterford and Lismore. While swimming in Tramore on July 11th, 1803, he had a fit and died. (ref. Daire Keogh).

J

JACOB, WILLIAM BEALE (1825-1902) Member of the Waterford Quaker community who opened a bakery at Bridge Street, Waterford, with his wife Hannah, and his brother Robert, in the late 1800s and started making biscuits. In 1851 he moved to Peter Street, Dublin. An inovative process based partly on a moving production line led to increased sales and exports to England where a factory was established in Liverpool. In 1883 Jacobs became a private limited company, and in 1928 became a public company. (Ref. R. S. Harrison)

JOHN (1167-1216) King of England. Youngest and favourite son of Henry 11, who, in 1177 created him "Dominus Hiberniae", thereby making him a permanent overlord of the Irish barons. He visited Waterford with a considerable army in 1185 at the age of 18 and alienated the citizens with his insolence and loutish manner. In England his behaviour is said to have hastened his father's death, and he did everything in his power to prevent his brother Richard (The Lionheart) from returning from captivity in the Holy Land to take his rightful throne. Conducted wars and intrigues over the English domain. Visited Ireland and Waterford again in 1210, mainly to disipline the Norman barons and re-inforce his rule as Lord of Ireland but also, since the death of Richard in 1199, as king of England. In 1215 he granted Waterford a charter of incorporation which conferred important and significant trading rights, including a virtual monoply on all goods carried to the area by sea. It also made Waterford a city or borough. In 1214 he was defeated by the French, and in 1215 he had to conceed to the demands of his barons at Runnymede, and sign the Magna Carta (or Great Charter) which gave them many rights, particularly that of individual liberty. Although these rights were confined to the aristocracy at the time, the Magna Carta laid the ground rules for those who later demanded democratic government and rights for all. King John left his name on many streets and places in Waterford. John's Hill, Johnstown, John's Bridge and John's

Street, when linked with Passage Road, may indicate a "route de roi" , or royal road, taken by King John on one or both occasions when he visited Waterford.

JORDAN, DOROTHEA (or DOROTHY) (1762-1816) Actress. Born in Waterford, the illegitimate child of Grace Phillips and Francis Bland. She first appeared on the stage in Dublin at the Crow Street Theatre (1777) where she played Phoebe in William Shakespeare's "As you Like It". She later played in Waterford and Cork, but was seduced by her manager, Richard Daly. She fled to Leeds with her mother, and changing her name to Mrs Jordan, played Calista and other parts on the York circuit under the management of Tate Wilkinson from 1782 - 1785. In 1785 made her debut at Drury Lane as Peggy in "The Country Girl" and continued to act there and at the Haymarket Theatre in various parts until 1809. Acted at Covent Garden from 1811 to 1814, Lady Teazle being her last performance. She was highly praised by Hazlitt, Lamb, and Leigh Hunt. She had a daughter by Richard Daly and four other children by Sir Richard Ford. She was for many years the mistress of the Duke of Clarence, later William IV, and bore him five sons and five daughters, all of whom took the name of Fitzclarence. According to some , she was often ill-treated by the duke but was quite prepared to stand up for herself. The duke gave her an allowance of £1,000 per annum, and when he tried to reduce it she sent him the the the bottom part of a play bill reading "no money returned after the rising of the curtain". She retired to St Cloud in France in 1815 and died on July 3rd 1816. She is buried in the cemetery at St Cloud.

JOY, DEREK (1944-1997) Musician and showband leader whose "Derek Joy Showband" was very popular all over Ireland in the Sixties. Members of his band included Earl Jordan and D. J. Curtin who later formed his own band, and later still joined Brendan Bowyer's Big Eight. The Derek Joy Showband went on to do extremely well in the USA and Mexico, although by then Derek Joy himself had returned to Waterford where he prefered to sing the blues in cabaret by night and return to his old job at Waterford Crystal by day. Throughout his life, he enjoyed the respect and affection of both his fans and his colleagues.

K

KEAN, Charles John (1811-1868) Actor. Born at Colebeck Street, Waterford, on Jan 18th 1811. Second son of actor Edmund Kean. Educated at Eton. At 16, his parents' marriage broke up (probably due to the "drunkeness and ostentation" of his father) and he took to the stage, appearing at Drury Lane as Young Norval in 1827. Played the Haymarket Theatre as Romeo in "Romeo and Juliet" and as other parts in 1829. Was a successful Richard 111 in New York, 1830. He later made up with his father and acted as Iago to his father's Othello at Covent Garden in 1833. His father died shortly afterwards. Later played in Hamburg, re-visited America in 1839 and 1846, and visited Australia, America and Jamaica 1863 - 66. In 1851 he took over the management of the Princess's Theatre in London and undertook numerous extravagant and spectacular revivals which unfortunately led to financial losses. He remained immensly popular and in 1859 a public banquet was held in his honour. In 1842 he married an Irish actress, Ellen Tree, in Dublin, and she travelled with him all over the world. He last appeared on stage in Liverpool in 1867, and died at Queensborough Terrace, Chelsea, on January 22nd, 1868.

KEANE, JOHN (1920-1991) All-Ireland winning hurler and All-Ireland winning coach. Spent most of his working life with Samuel Morris Builder's Providers on the Manor. Lived at St Johns Park. Joined Mount Sion in 1935 and within a few years had become one of Waterford's top hurlers. Said to be one of the few players to match Mick Mackey, he played centre-forward in the All-Ireland Final of 1948 in which Waterford beat Dublin (6-7 to 4-2). Although goalie Jim Ware captained the team, John Keane (according to veteran hurling writer Raymond Smith) "was the general who, Rommel-like, masterminded Waterford's surge to the title". In 1959 John Keane once more accompanied a Waterford team to the All-Ireland, this time as trainer, to beat Kilkenny (3-12 to 1-10). The other members of the 1959 All-

· Ireland winning team were:

	Ned Power	
	(Tallow)	
Joe Harney	Austin Flynn	John Barron
(Ballydurn)	(Abbeyside)	(De La Salle)
Mick Lacey	Martin Og Morrissey	Jackie Condon
(Cappoquin)	(Mount Sion)	(Erin's Own)
	Seamus Power	Phil Grimes
	(Mount Sion)	(Mount Sion)
Larry Guinan	Tom Cheasty	Frankie Walsh, capt.
(Mount Sion)	(Ballyduff)	(Mount Sion)
Charlie Ware	Donal Whelan	John Kiely
(Eirin's Own)	(Abbeyside)	(Dungarvan)

Substitutes; Tom Cunningham (Dungarvan); Mick Flannelly (Mount Sion); Freddie O'Brien (Mount Sion); Paudie Casey (Ballygunner); Michael O'Connor (Cappoquin); Tom Coffey (Tourin); Joe Coady (Erin's Own).

During his hurling career, John Keane played with Mount Sion in ten County Championship wins (he was captain for eight of them). He played for Munster for nine years and won seven Railway Cup medals.

KEANE, John (1781-1844) first Baron Keane. Lieutenant-General. Born in Belmont House, Cappoquin, Co. Waterford, second son of Sir John Keane, Bt. Entered British Army at 12 years of age and had reached the rank of major-general at 33. Saw service in Egypt, Martinique, Vittoria, and the Pyrenees in the Napoleonic Wars. During the Anglo-American War of 1812 he directed the landing of the first troops at the Battle of New Orleans, and was severely wounded. He was knighted in 1815. Commanded troops in Jamaica, 1823-30, and was promoted Lieutenant-General (1830). Commander-in-Chief Bombay, 1834-39. Captured Ghuznee and occupied Kabul, 1839. His treatment of the native people in this last campaign was harsh, and his methods were widely censured. Nevertheless, he received a peerage and a pension.

KEANE, Sir JOHN Bart (1873-1938) Fifth baronet, of Cappoquin House, Cappoquin, Co Waterford. Served as a

captain in the Royal Artillery before becoming private secretary
to the governor of Ceylon. Served in the Boer War (1900) and
was mentioned in despatches. Succeeded to the baronetcy in
1892 and was high sheriff of Waterford in 1911. Returned to the
British Army on the outbreak of the First World War with the
rank of major and served with distinction (awarded the DSO).
After the War of Independence he served the Irish Free State in
the Senate for several years. During the Civil War his house at
Belmont was set on fire and destroyed. He was one of the leaders
of the Waterford Farmers Association in the 1923 conflict
between farmers and their workers, and witnessed the gradual
reduction of the Keane estates as the new Land Acts enabled
tenants to buy out their holdings. As a senator he fought for
freedom of speech (he was against censorship) and freedom of
assembly (he condemned the banning of the blueshirts). In the
former he was supported by Senator W. B. Yates. (ref. Patrick
Power)

KEANE, SIR RICHARD Bart (1780-1855)   Second baronet
(eldest son of Sir John Keane, Bart). Of Cappoquin House,
Cappoquin, Co Waterford. A lieutenant-colonel in the Waterford
Militia he was also MP for Waterford (1832-35). In 1831 he
leased 470 acres of mountain land to the Trappist monks for 99
years at a nominal rent. They reclaimed much of the land and
built the famous monastery of Mount Melleray. When
questioned in 1845 about the transaction he said "I conceived I
was not violating any law in giving land to persons whose
improvement in agriculture I had known would be an example
to all the country. I marked out a space consisting of 470 acres
andI gave it to them for 99 years. It had been a nest of sheep
stealers who absolutely plundered the whole of the tenantry and
is now in the most highly improved state". During the famine
Sir Richard used his influence to have a substantial stone bridge
(Victoria Bridge) built over the Blackwater river at Cappoquin
as relief work. (ref S.& S. Murphy)

KEANE, MOLLY (1905-1996) Novelist and playwright. Born
Mary Nesta Skrine in County Kildare. Of an Anglo-Irish
background, she was educated by governesses until the age of
fourteen when she was sent as a boarder to The French School,

Bray, where she was very lonely. This isolation led her to start
writing and she wrote her first novel "The Knight of the
Cheerful Countenance", at the age of seventeen. It was sold to
Mills and Boon, for £75, in 1926. This novel, and the nine which
followed, were written under the pseudonym "M. J. Farrell" (a
name seen over a pub) because writers were sneered at among
her foxhunting friends. She wrote several successful plays
which were directed in the West End by John Gielgud, including
"Spring Meeting" (1938), "Ducks and Drakes" (1942) and
"Treasure Hunt" (1949). In 1938 she married Robert Lumley
Keane and had two daughters. His sudden death (in 1946) at
the age of 36 was devastating, and this along with the failure of
her play "Dazzling Prospect" (1961) led to a long period of
"creative silence". In the late seventies, she began writing
again, under her own name, and produced "Good Behaviour"
(1981) which was shortlisted for the Booker Prize, followed by
"Time after Time" (1983), "Loving and Giving" (1988) and
"Conversation Piece" (1991). Most of her books were set in the
beautiful country houses of the Anglo-Irish, but were often
quietly critical of the sometimes insular and stultifying aspects
of this society. She also produced a popular volume of hunting
reminiscences, "Red Letter Days", illustrated by the famous
equestrian artist, "Snaffles". Molly Keane spent almost 40 years
of her life in her beloved Dysert, Ardmore, Co. Waterford, where
she died in 1996.

KEATING, GEOFFREY Dr. (1570-1650) Bishop and scholar.
Born at Burges, Co Tipperary. Author of "Foras Feasa ar
Éirinn", a history of Ireland up to the English invasion, written
(in Irish, c.1630) to repudiate what he though were the
Anglophile writings of Geraldus Cambrensis, Spenser, and
others. Though not printed until the eighteenth century, it was
for many years widely circulated in manuscript. When he died
he was buried in the 17th Century church at Tubrid, Co
Waterford which he had caused to be built in honour of of St.
Ciaran.

KELLY, EDMUND WALSH (d.1940) Land agent, actuary and
amateur genealogist, who, during his long period of service with
Waterford Savings Bank collected an enormous amount of social

and statistical information from church, municipal and national sources, and from painstakingly recording the burial information from over seventy graveyards. His most important contributions to the historical records of Waterford come from items he had transcribed from the records held in the Public Record Office in the Four Courts just before they were occupied by the Republicans in 1922 and subsequently largely destroyed. These include the religious census of 1766 covering parts of Waterford, Portnascully and Killotteran, and large parts of the census returns for 1821, 1831, 1841 and 1851. In addition, he had collected details from hundreds of wills and other documents. (Julian Walton Decies/XXXV)

KELLY, KITTY (1909-1986) Niece of Edmund Walsh Kelly, with whom she had shared a passion for local history (mainly of south Kilkenny) and from whom, on his death, she took over the responsibility of sorting, typing and filing the enormous amount of information he had collected. She herself added much important work to his collection. She was a founder-member of the Old Waterford Society, and served as Hon. Secretary 1963-68, and Hon. Treasurer 1970-78. She worked for many years at the firm of Henry Gallwey & Co., Gladstone Street.

KELLY, PATRICK, Waterford-born racing cyclist who won the South-East Ireland Cup in 1883 and cycled, both socially and competitively, all over Ireland and on the Continent, writing an amusing diary of his experiences. He died while cycling in France and is buried there. A niece of his lived on the Priest's Road in Tramore up to quite recently. (ref. Muiris O Ceallaig)

KELLY, SEAN (b.1956) champion cyclist. Born in Waterford, and raised at Curraghduff, Co.Waterford. Won Irish Junior Championship in 1972 and first won professionally in 1977. He was enormously successful from 1984 to 1989, winning literally dozens of races including 12 one-day classics, and was generally regarded as the world's leading cyclist at this time. He was the World Cup winner in 1989. Despite his best efforts he failed to win the Tour de France although he won five stages between 1978 and 1982 and wore the yellow jersey in 1983. He won the Paris-Nice stage race seven times in a row - an amazing achievement.   He was granted the Freedom of the City of Waterford in 1986.

KENNEALLY, WILLIAM BRENDAN (b. 1955) Politician. Born in Waterford, the son of Billy Kenneally, TD and grandson of William Kenneally, TD. Educated at St. Declans National School, De La Salle College, and Waterford Regional Technical College. Having trained in accountancy at Chambers & Halley, Waterford (now Ernst & Young), he worked with Fyffes from 1978 to 1989. He was a member of Waterford Corporation 1985-92, and mayor of Waterford 1988 - 89. In 1992 he was elected to Dáil Éireann for Fianna Fáil and made Minister of State, Dept. of Tourism, Transport and Communications. He was re-elected in 1997. In opposition he has been spokesman for Energy and Natural Resources (1994-97). He has been a member of the Council of Europe (1992-94) and is Vice-chairman of the Oireachtas Committee on Heritage and the Irish Language (1997 to date). His grandfather, William (Billy) Kenneally, was mayor of Waterford in 1945/46 and officiated at the granting of the freedom of the city to Eamon De Valera in January 1946. He was elected to the Dail in 1952 and held his seat until 1961. He died suddenly at the county hurling final in Walsh Park in 1963. Brendan's father, also Billy Kenneally (b. 1926), was a member of the Dail from 1965 to 1982, of the Senate from February 1982 to November 1982, and was mayor of Waterford from 1976 to 1977 and from 1984 to 1985. He was opposition front bench spokesman on Fisheries from 1973 to 1975 and was chairman of the Fianna Fáil Parliamentary Party for a number of years from 1977. A member of Waterford County Council for many years since 1964. President of Erin's Own GAA Club. He continues to be active in local affairs as a member of the Waterford Harbour Board (1998).

KENNEDY, GERALDINE (b. 1951) Journalist and former T D. Born in Tramore on Sept. 7th 1951 and raised on the family farm at Glenbower House, parish of Ballyneal, near Carrick-on-Suir. Her father, James Kennedy, was a well-known cattle farmer who died in 1977. She and her three sisters were educated at Sacred Heart of Mary Convent, Waterford. In 1968 she completed the Leaving Cert. and, on a whim, attended the School of

Journalism, Rathmines. After completing the course she spent six months in the Kilkenny office of *The Munster Express*, and then, over a period of years, worked for *The Cork Examiner*, *The Irish Times*, *The Sunday Tribune* and *The Sunday Press*. She was the first woman in Ireland to work as a political correspondent and while working in this position with *The Sunday Tribune* in 1982, her telephone was tapped by the Gardai for six months on foot of a warrant signed by the Minister of Justice, Sean Doherty. New grounds for the tapping - "national security"- had to be invented, though in reality, the minister was trying to locate alleged cabinet "leaks". A national scandal ensued, the Garda Commissioner resigned, the tapes were published, and in 1986 Ms Kennedy won her case (for invasion of privacy) in the High Court. She represented Dun Laoghaire in the Dáil from 1987 to 89 as a member of the Progressive Democrats. Three of Geraldine Kennedy's uncles (two of whom were twins) on her father's side, were ordained into the Cistercian Order. Fr. Gerard Kennedy became abbot of the monastry at Collon, Co. Louth. Fr. Mark Kennedy spent many years at Mount Melleray where he managed the farm.

KILLEA, MR. Editor of *The Waterford Chronicle* in 1848, he was a fierce nationalist who advertised the sale of guns, recommending their purchase, and undertaking to arm 200,000 revolutionaries. He also painted his house green as a rallying point for rebels !.

KIRWAN, PERCY, Athlete, of Kilmacthomas, Co. Waterford. He was British champion Long-jumper in 1910, 1911 and 1912.

KYNE, THOMAS A. (1905-1981) Trade unionist and politician. Born Dungarvan, Co. Waterford. Educated CBS Dungarvan. Began involvement with trade unions in late thirties. Became full-time official of the ATGWU. Member of Dungarvan Urban Council from 1942 of which he became chairman for 20 years. Member of Waterford County Council from 1945 and member of Waterford City Council from 1955 to 1960. Elected Waterford TD for Labour in 1948 and in each election thereafter until defeated in 1969. Was elected again in 1973 but retired in 1977. Labour Spokesman on Health 1957-1969. Chairman of the

Labour parliamentary party 1973-1977. Lived at Abbeyside, Dungarvan.

L

LEDINGHAM, JAMES (b. 1985) A member of Ring-Old Parish Athletic Club, he won the All-Ireland, under 13 Cross-Country title at Kilcoole, Co. Wicklow on December 6th 1997.

LEDINGHAM, Capt. JOHN (b.1958) International Showjumper. Born at Clashmore, Co. Waterford on June 26th 1958. Educated at the local National School and at Youghal CBS. At the age of 17 he became an army cadet and spent two years at the Military College before joining the Army School of Equitation. He competed on his first Nation's Cup team in 1980, and to date has represented Ireland on approximately 53 Nation's Cup teams. On five seperate occasions he has been a member of the winning Aga Khan Trophy team. Between 1987 and 1991 he won 5 Puissances in the RDS in Dublin. Other major achievements include: Competing at Olympic Games in Seoul, Korea (1988); Irish National Speed Champion (1989); National Champion (1990); Winner of the Hickstead Derby (1984, 1994 and 1995); winner of the Hickstead Speed Derby (1993, 1994 and 1995). In 1997, amongst other achievements in a very busy year, he won the Hurricane Cup at Calgary, Alberta, the Viceroy Derby at Monterey, Mexico, and the Nation's Cup at Zagreb, Aachen, and Dublin. He lives at Bective, Navan, Co. Meath.

LITTLE, PATRICK JOHN (1884-1963) Fianna Fail TD for Waterford from 1927 to 1953. Born Co Dublin, son of P. F. Little, a former Premier of Newfoundland who had returned to Ireland to support Parnell. Educated at Clongowes and UCD. Qualified as solicitor. Fought with the Volunteers in 1916 and was arrested. Opposed treaty and was jailed by the Free State forces. Editor of *An Phoblacht*. Founder Member of Fianna Fáil. Minister for External Affairs 1933-39. Minister for Posts and Telegraphs 1939-48. Was a friend of W.F. Watt and at his request became President of Waterford Music Club. Lived at Clonlea, Sandyford, Co. Dublin.

LOMBARD, PETER (1554-1625) Archbishop and scholar. Born in Waterford. Educated at Westminster, Oxford and at Louvain University. DD, (1594); provost of Cambrai Cathedral (1594). While in Rome he was made Archbishop of Armagh and Primate of All Ireland (1601-1625) but never returned to Ireland. Author of "De Regno Hiberniae, Sanctorum Insula Commentarius" which supports O'Neill's Rebellion as a defense of the Catholic faith. It was published posthumously in 1632 but banned by Charles 1.

LONERGAN, DECLAN (b.1969) Champion cyclist. Born in Waterford and raised at The Folly. Educated at Scoile Lorcáin and the Technical School, Slieverue. Apart from Sean Kelly, he is the only man in Ireland to have won a much sought-after World Cup Medal. He achieved this distinction in 1996, in Havana, Cuba. In 1987 he set a new Irish track record at Besancon, France, and for the next nine years he raced in Ireland, France, Luxemburg, Belgium, the United States, Canada, Colombia and Cuba. During this time he was consistantly successful, with 57 wins, 37second-placings and 27 third-placings. To the great disappointment of himself and his supporters, he failed to do well in the Olympics of 1996, but close friends say a virus knocked him off form. He lives and trains in the USA.

LUMLEY, Captain JOSEPH (1863-1917) Master of the Waterford-based Steamer, "Coningbeg" which was sunk by a torpedo from a German submarine when returning from Liverpool on the night of December 17th 1917. Captain Lumley lost his life along with all 43 passengers and crew. Perhaps unknown to him, his son William died only hours before, when the other principal Waterford steamer, the S.S. "Formby", on which he was an officer, was sunk with all hands by the same submarine, U-62. The lives of many Waterford families were fatally entwined with the two ships. For example, well-known Waterford hurler, Jackie Condon of Woodstown, lost both his grandfathers, Thomas Condon on the S. S. "Formby", and Patrick Wall on the S. S. "Coningbeg". Also lost on the "Coningbeg" was Thomas Griffin of the well-known Griffin family of "Intacta Print". The "Coningbeg" was built in Scotland in 1903 for the Waterford Steamship Company and was originally named "*Clodagh*". When the Waterford Steamship Co. was acquired by the Clyde Shipping Co. in 1912 she was renamed "*Coningbeg*", and in the following year was completely refitted and modernised. She was 270 feet long, weighed 1278 tons gross and had a top speed of 16.5 knots.   Captain Lumley, one of the most experienced masters on the Irish Sea route, lived at 13 Percy Terrace, Waterford.   His family still live in the city. In 1997, eighty years after the double tragedy, a memorial was unveiled at Adelphi Quay by President Mary Robinson, attended by some of the descendants of those lost.

LUSBY, JIM (b. 1950) Author. Born and raised at 46 Gracedieu Road, Waterford. The Lusbys were an old Waterford Protestant family which originally came from England. His mother's maiden name was Kennedy, and his father worked in the old Flourmills in Ferrybank. He was educated at Mount Sion CBS and was first encouraged in his writing by a Christian Brother, the Irish language poet, Sean O' Cearbhaill.   At the age of 18 he left Waterford, initially to work in London as a labourer, but returned briefly in 1970 to sit the Leaving Cert. and avail of a local authority university grant.   Attended UCC from 1970 to 1975 (Ba and H. Dip. in Ed.) and spent a year studying for an MA but did not complete it as he felt the "academic study of Literature seemed arid".   Taught at Sandymount High School, Dublin, from 1975 to 1980, but resigned to give more time to writing while working at a wide range of odd jobs. His first published work was a short story, "Funerals", in New Irish Writing, edited by David Marcus (1977), which won a Hennessy Literary Award.   Over the following years, many other stories were published, most notably "The Gift", "Family Circles", and "Some Sort of Trouble at Home".   In the late eighties, he collaborated with Myles Dungan of RTE on a number of projects including the radio comedy series, "Stop, You're Killing Me!". They also founded a touring theatre group and co-wrote a crime thriller, "Snuff", set in RTE.   This attracted the attention of Jim's London agent, David O'Leary.   Jim Lusby has published the following books to date: "Making the Cut" (1995) set in Waterford and televised by RTE in 1997. "Flashback" (1996), the second in the Detective Carl McCadden series, also set in

Waterford, and "Kneeling at the Altar" (1998) also featuring Carl McCadden. Under the name of James Kennedy he has published "Armed and Dangerous" (1996) and "Silent City", (1998).

LYNCH, THADDEUS ("Teddy") (1901-1966) Politician and Mayor of Waterford. Born in Waterford. Educated at Mount Sion CBS and Newbridge College. Became a farmer and auctioneer. Member of Waterford City Council 1939-1966. Mayor of Waterford, 1949 and 1951. Was unsuccessful in his bid to be elected to the Dail in 1952, but was elected TD (FG) for Waterford in 1954, 1957, 1961 and 1965. Was married with two sons and a daughter and lived at Glendhu, Lower Grange, Waterford.

M

MAC CON MARA, Donnchad Rua (1715-1810) Poet, wanderer and rake. Born in Co. Clare. Sent to Rome to study for priesthood but expelled for misconduct and sent back to Ireland. Worked for a while as a schoolmaster at Sliabh gCua, near the Comeragh Mountains, in a school famed for its Irish poetry. Afterwards he wandered around Ireland and the continent, and there is evidence, particularly in his poetry, to suggest that he may have sailed from Waterford to Newfoundland, and spent some time there. In any event, at the age of 55, he returned to the Comeraghs penniless and in ill-health, and turned Protestant in order to qualify for the job of parish clerk at Rossmire. At last he seems to have settled down, and lived on to the extraordinary old age (considering the period and his lifestyle) of 95. His death was announced in The Freeman's Journal in October 1810 as that of "Denis MacNamara, commonly known by the name of Ruadh, or Redhead, the most celebrated of the modern bards". Amongst his poems were: "Eachtra Ghiolla an Amaráin", sometimes referred to as The Mock Aeneid, "Bán Cnoic Éireann Óigh", "Aodh O Ceallaigh", and "As I Was Walking One Evening Fair". He is buried in Newtown churchyard, Kilmacthomas. On the centenary of his death a gravestone was erected with subscriptions from the Waterford and South East Archaeological Society.

MACKEY, PATRICK Local writer and historian who was active in the nineteen-eighties. For many years, he was the only Waterford writer producing local history booklets and guides. He has produced a number of books and publications, some of them commissioned by Waterford Corporation, dealing with Waterford's history. They include: "By Hook or by Crooke"(1983); "Reginald's Tower and the Story of Waterford" (1980), "Talk of the Town", and "Selected Walks Through Waterford" (1981)

McCARTHY, BILLY (b. 1954) Controller of Programmes, WLR

FM. Born in Waterford. Educated at Mount Sion CBS; Oaklands College, Mount Merrion; UCD; St. Patricks College, Maynooth; Gregorian College, Rome; Boston College, Massachusetts. Was Director of Religious Education in the Waterford diocese from 1984 to 1989. In 1989 he joined WLR - FM as broadcaster where he hosts an important current affairs programme (Deise AM) on weekday mornings.

McCARTHY, THOMAS (b. 1954) Poet. Born in Cappoquin, Co. Waterford. Attended UCC. While at university he founded the Poetry Workshop in 1975. He has published collections of poetry, including "The First Convention" which won the 1977 Kavanagh Award.

McGRATH, PAT. Captain of the under-21 hurling team that beat Clare in the 1974 provincial final by a score of 2-5 to 1-3. The other members of the team were: W. Ryan, F. McCarthy, M.Flynn, K. Ryan, L. O'Brien, J. Galvin, E. Ryan, P. Egan, (P. McGrath), T. Casey, L. Power, P. O'Keefe, B. Mansfield, M. McNamara, P. Moore. A member of Mount Sion club, Pat McGrath had been elected Waterford Hurler of the Year in 1973 at the age of 20.

MAHONY, JAMES (1828 - 1907) The last High Constable of Waterford to reside in Reginald's Tower. The title was rather grand, but in fact the position was mainly ceremonial and the duties were more like those of a police constable. Nevertheless he received a long service medal from Queen Victoria. He lived for over 30 years in Reginald's Tower, and when he died his daughter lived on in the tower up to the nineteen-forties. A grand-nephew remembers visiting the daughter when she was an old lady, and how she had to laboriously climb the narrow, winding staircase to her gloomy apartment, which she tried to brighten up by putting flower-pots in the small window openings. These can be seen in some old photographs of the tower.

MALCOLMSON, DAVID (1765-1844) Quaker corn merchant of Portlaw, Waterford. In 1825, having made a fortune in the Napoleonic Wars, he went on to establish a cotton factory at

Strongbow's tombstone in Christchurch Cathedral, Dublin.

*John Palliser and James Hector in 1860
(courtesy of Alberta Provincial Library)*

Thomas Francis Meagher
(As Brigadier-General of the Irish Brigade, 1861-4)

Fieldmarshal Lord Roberts near the end of his life.

John E. Redmond

Captain Joseph Lumley

Richard Mulcahy (on right) with Michael Collins

Putting Hounds into cover at Halfway House, Tramore – The late Forties, Joe Power and Fergus Power.
(Photo courtesy of Waterford Beagles)

Carmel O'Byrne

Captain R.J. Farrell

Fintan O'Carroll

"B" Company, 46th Battalion, L.D.F (Competition Team) May 6th 1945
Paddy Walsh, Jack Ryan, Ben hart, John Dower, Mattie Keane, Tim Mulhall,
Andy Murphy, O. Chestnut, T.M. Fewer, Pat Maddock, Billy Kelly, Michael Dunphy,
John Hearne, Eddie Fanning

Waterford All-Ireland Champions 1948
Back Row: M. Hayes M. Healy, M. Hickey, E. Carew, A. Fleming, J. Allen, V. Baston, J. Keane, D. Powr, T. Curran, J. Murphy, P. Neville, W. Galvin, J. Galvin.
Front Row: J. Cusack, J. Goode, E. Daly, K. O'Connor, J. Ware (Capt.), C. Moylan, M. Feeney, P. Waters, J. O'Connor, L. Fanning.

Charmian Hill

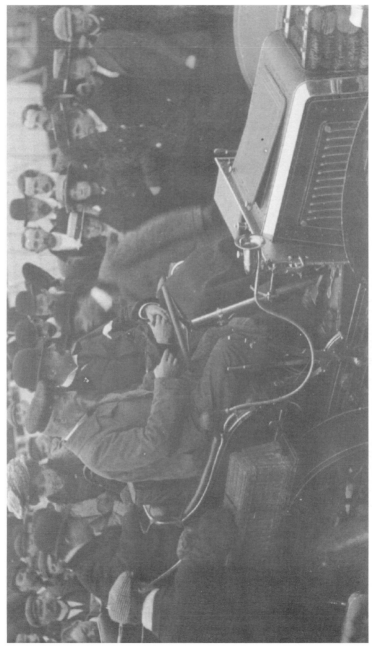

W.G.D. Goff (with beard) in one of his early motor cars

Father Luke Wadding

Mayfield, Portlaw, which was to become the"biggest industrial employer in Ireland outside Belfast" (E. O'Connor) At its height in the 1850s, it employed 1800 people and turned the village of Portlaw into an ultra-modern and prosperous 'factory town', although the factory itself was considered overcrowded and stuffy by the almost powerless health inspectors of the day. The family then went into shipbuilding, gradually building bigger and better ships and applying the lessons they had learned in the cotton factory. In 1844, the year that David died, his son Joseph opened the Neptune Iron Works, near what is now Waterpark College. This yard built steam-powered iron-hulled ships, the first of them being the "Neptune", which was built to trade between London and St Petersburg . The yard built over forty steamships, from small colliers to large ocean-going ships, before it closed in 1890. One of the biggest was the "Odessa" (1898 tons), built in 1857 for the Odessa Steamship Company.

By 1860 Malcolmson Bros. was one of the most powerful companies in the British Isles, with important and often controlling interests in the corn and cotton industries, shipbuilding, steamship lines, fish exporting and coal mines. The commercial success of the family at the time was compared to that of the Rothschilds. According to Bill Irish, it was once claimed in the House of Commons that they were the biggest ship-owners in the world , with 90 ships registered in Waterford. When Joseph died in 1858, his younger brother William took over the reins, but problems lay ahead. There were losses at sea and the American Civil War meant a shortage of raw cotton. Meanwhile the family built fine houses around the county, including Clodagh and Woodlock in Portlaw and what is now The Haven Hotel in Dunmore East (formerly the Villa Marina). When Joseph's widow Charlotte, and his Aunt Rachel, decided to cash in their shares it was the beginning of the end. In 1867 Joseph's son David died and his widow withdrew almost £200,000 from the business. The family struggled on for a few years by selling off their assets, until, in 1877, they went into bankruptcy. Their generosity is remembered in Dunmore East, however, where they left parkland and woods to the community, and where the Fishermen's Hall was built with funds donated by Mrs David Malcolmson in memory of her son Joseph. (ref. Bill Irish (1992), Emmet O'Connor (1989) & Ernest Anderson(1932))

MANAHAN, ANNA, Actress. Born in Waterford and educated at the Mercy Convent. She developed a love of acting at an early age and was encouraged in her ambition by the Mercy Convent nuns for whom she says she has the greatest admiration. She was accepted for audition for a scholarship by the Royal Academy of Dramatic Art in London but was forbidden to travel by her parents as London was at the time being bombed by the Luftwaffe. She joined the Waterford Dramatic Society and took part in local dramatics before joining the Mooney School of Acting in Dublin which sent her out with the No.1 fit-up company of Sheila Ward and John McMahon. Here she acted with Seamus Brannock, Geoffrey Golden, Patrick McGee, Wilfred Bramble (of TV's Steptoe & Son) and many others. She attended the Gabriel Pascal Film School and did a season at the Mercury Theatre, London. There she met Phyllis Ryan and began a long personal and professional friendship. She also acted with Liam Redmond. Later she came back to Waterford to look after her sister Billie, who died at the age of 28. Auditioned by Barry Cassin, she joined the 37 Theatre where she met her husband, Carl O'Kelly. She was then auditioned by Hilton Edwards and was accepted for the Gate Theatre. She married Carl in 1955, but after only ten months of marriage he contracted polio and died while they were on a trip with the Gate Theatre to Egypt. He is buried in Alexandria. In May 1957 she played Serafina in Tennessee William's "Rose Tattoo" which was produced by Alan Simpson in the tiny Pike Theatre in Dublin. The play was viewed with suspicion by the authorities, and when an envelope appeared on the stage one night during the performance, the police claimed it was a condom. Consequently, the theatre was closed and Simpson was charged with indecency. Nine months of proceedings failed to bring about a conviction but the Pike Theatre was financially ruined. Anna's career continued in Ireland and England in films and on the stage, and then followed a period of twenty years acting in the United States (including an appearance at Carnegie Hall) interspersed with working visits back to Ireland. John B. Keane is said to have written "Big Maggie" especially for her in 1969. In the eighties she returned to Ireland and worked with The Druid and Red Kettle Theatre Companies. In the nineties she received great acclaim for her performances in "Happy Birthday

Dear Alice" (1994), "The Old Ladies Guide to Survival" (1996) "The Crucible" (1996) and two parts of the Leenane trilogy with the Druid Theatre, (1997). In 1998, in New York, she won a Tony Award as Best Featured Actress for her part in the Broadway production of "The Beauty Queen of Leenane" by Martin McDonagh.

MATTHEWS, JOHN ALAN (b. 1946) Professional footballer. Born in Coventry, England. Played soccer for Coventry, Limerick and Waterford. The holder of seven League of Ireland Championship medals (six for Waterford, one for Limerick), he is Waterford United's leading goal scorer to date. With 156 goals,he was League of Ireland's leading Goal Scorer. In 1989-90, he managed Waterford United to a 1st Division Championship. He is a qualified FAI referee, and now works part-time as a sports commentator with WLR - FM. Lives at Sweetbriar Lawn, Tramore.

MAY, Sir JAMES (d. 1798) Baronet, High Sheriff of County Waterford in 1752, and MP 1759-98. A descendant of Sir Algernon May who lived at Mayfield (originally Rockett's Castle) in Clonegam parish. The village of Mayfield later became known as Portlaw. His mother was Letitia Ponsonby, daughter of Viscount Duncannon. A memorial to the May family was erected in the old Christ Church Cathedral in 1686, and when the cathedral was demolished towards the end of the 18th century on the doubtful grounds that it was 'dangerous', the memorial was placed in the present cathedral.

MEAGHER, THOMAS FRANCIS (1823-1867) "Meagher of the Sword". Nationalist leader and soldier. His father, Thomas Meagher, one of the richest men in Waterford, married Alicia Quan, daughter of a partner in the Waterford merchant firm of Wyse, Cushin and Quan. The marriage took place in the Meagher family home on the Quay in Waterford, where Thomas Francis was born on August 3rd, 1823. Two years later his father sold the house to Charles Bianconi and the Meagher family moved to Derrynane House on The Mall. The house of his birth became the Waterford terminus for the Bianconi 'long car' coach transport system; Commins Commercial Hotel, and later still, after complete re-construction and the addition of two storeys, the Granville Hotel. Young Meagher was educated at Clongowes Wood College and Stoneyhurst College, the traditional English public school for young Catholic gentlemen. He returned to Ireland in 1843 and initially considered service in the Austrian army, but decided instead to go to Dublin and study for the Bar. There he met the writers of "The Nation" and "discovered his country, whose history had been debarred in his education" (Griffith). In his late teens he had admired Daniel O'Connell, who had visited Clongowes Wood and had praised an article by Meagher. In September 1843 he and his father attended one of O'Connell's 'monster' meetings at Lismore and he made his first important speech. He was just 20, and O'Connell clapped him on the shoulder, saying, "well done, young Ireland". Meagher became an ardent supporter of the Repeal movement and a founder of the Irish Confederation. He became an eloquent political speaker and often drew large crowds to hear him at Conciliation Hall in Dublin. In a speech to the Repeal Association in 1846 he likenened the sword to a sacred weapon, which led Thackeray to call him "Meagher of the Sword". However, he disliked Dublin society for what he described as, "its pretentious aping of English taste, ideas and fashions...and its utter want of all sound love of country". He stood for election unsuccessfully in Waterford in 1848, (he was beaten by Henry Winston Barron), and in the same year was arrested after the abortive rising lead by William Smith O'Brien. He was sentenced to death but was reprieved and committed instead to penal servitude for life in Van Diemen's Land. In 1852 he escaped to the United States and over the next eight years became a member of the New York bar, a journalist, a publisher and one of the best-known lecturers in the country. He helped John Mitchell, the author of "Jail Journal", to found *"The Citizen"* newspaper, but they grew apart when the Civil War started and Mitchell became a champion of the Southern states while Meagher not only supported the North but founded the Irish Brigade, and fought with them as their Brigadier General. He was not afraid to lead from the front and at the Battle of Sharpsburg (Sept. 17th 1862), he had his horse shot from under him and was carried unconcious from the field. After the war he became acting governor of Montana territory. On the night of

July 1st 1867, while travelling on the Missouri, he disappeared overboard in what is thought to have been an accident. He is credited with having introduced the Tricolour as the National flag of Ireland. It is believed to have been flown for the first time from the former Wolfe Tone Meeting House on The Mall, in Waterford (opposite the Town Hall) in March 1848. While in Van Diemen's Land he married Catherine Bennett, the daughter of a free settler. When he escaped to America his wife arranged to follow him after the birth of their baby. Unfortunately, the infant died shortly after birth and was buried in Tasmania. Catherine travelled to Ireland where she was received with affection and enthusiasm. She then went to America to be with Meagher but became ill and returned to Ireland less than a year later to be cared for by the Meagher family. The illness proved to be fatal and Catherine died in May 1854. She is buried in the Meagher family vault at Faithlegge. On November 14th 1855 Meagher married Elizabeth Townsend, the daughter of a wealthy New York merchant.

MINARDS, Captain CHARLES (1851-1917) Captain of SS *"Formby"*, the Waterford steamer sunk in the Irish Sea by the German submarine, U-62 on the night of December 15th 1917. All 39 people on board were lost. Only one body, that of the stewardess, Annie O'Callaghan, was found. Within 48 hours, the sistership of the *"Formby"*, the SS *"Coningbeg"*, under the command of Captain Joseph Lumley (q.v.), was also torpedoed and sunk by U-62, with the loss of all 44 souls on board. Captain Minards lived at No. 56 St Declan's Terrace, Waterford. A memorial to the *"Formby"* and the *"Coningbeg"* was unveiled at Adelphi quay in 1997 by President Mary Robinson.

MOORE, JOHN (1763-1799) In the Old Graveyard of Ballygunner, where it had lain forgotten for a hundred years, is a tombstone inscribed "Here lies the body of John Moore Esq., of Ashbrook in County Mayo, who died in the City of Waterford on the 6th Day of December 1799 aged 36 years" John Moore was the eldest son of George Moore of Moore Hall and an ancestor of the novelist George Augustus Moore (1852-1933). During the Insurrection of 1798, newly in command of a body of rebel troops, he had made contact with the French forces under

General Humbert. Humbert quickly appointed him to be the first President of Connacht. In the fighting that followed, Moore was captured. He was dragged from prison to prison, until, possibly en route to England, he is thought to have died in the Royal Oak Inn, just off Broad Street in Waterford. In recent times, the remains of John Moore have been exhumed and returned to his native Mayo, where they were re-interred in a grave beside the 1798 Memorial in Castlebar, on which he is described as "the first president of Ireland". (ref. Maeve Friel)

MORAN, DAVID PATRICK (1871-1936) Journalist and author. Born in Co. Waterford and educated at Castleknock College, Dublin. A member of the London branch of the Gaelic League and Irish Literary Society, he returned to Ireland to found and edit *"The Leader"* (1900) in which he expressed his support for a form of Gaelic nationalism which would eschew any similarities with the English political system. The paper gave great support to the Irish-Ireland movement and for a time won wide circulation. He did not regard the writings of W. B. Yeats and others in the Irish literary revival movement as being representative of the true Gael. Amongst his other works were, "The Philosophy of Irish Ireland" (1905) and "Tom O'Kelly", a novel also published in 1905.

MORGAN. A name associated in Waterford with horse-racing for over 100 years. At the turn of the century no less than four Morgan brothers rode in one Grand National (unfortunately without being placed). They were Frank, Dick, William and Reese Morgan. In 1904 Frank rode the winner of the Irish Derby, "Royal Arch". In 1919 Tommy Morgan, at the age of 13 and weighing only 4 stone 7 lbs, rode in the Great Metropolitan at Epsom. He was still enjoying retirement in England at the age of 91. In 1929, Tommy and Danny Morgan both rode in the Grand National. Danny Morgan went on to win the Cheltenham Gold Cup in 1938 on "Morse Code" and during his career as a jockey rode for three kings of England. One of the successful 'royal' horses was 'Marconi', which retired to grass in Waterford. In 1959 Danny was the trainer of "Roddy Owen", which won the Cheltenham Gold Cup of that year. His brother, Dick Morgan, is still involved in the bloodstock export and insurance business.

MULCAHY, RICHARD (1886-1971) Revolutionary, soldier and politician, and General Officer in Command, Irish Army. Born in Waterford. Educated at CBS Mount Sion and Thurles. Followed his father into the Postal Services and worked in Thurles, Bantry and Dublin. He joined the Volunteers soon after they were formed in 1913. He fought in the 1916 Rising under Thomas Ashe at Ashbourne, Co Dublin. Afterwards he was arrested and interned at Frongoch until he was released in the general amnesty of 1917. He immediately rejoined his comrades and quickly became chief-of-staff of the IRA. Elected MP for Clontarf division, 1918. In 1919 he married Josephine Ryan, a sister of Sean T. O'Kelly's wife. He supported the Treaty of 1921 and became General Officer Commanding the forces of the Provisional Government during the Civil War. He was elected TD in 1922 and at all subsequent elections (except for 1937 and 1943) and retained his seat until he retired in 1961. He first represented Dublin constituencies but from 1944 he was elected in Tipperary. During the Civil War he worked closely with Michael Collins and was involved with him in the supplying of arms to the IRA in Northern Ireland. He became Commander-in Chief of the Army after Collins's death and conducted a vigorous campaign against the anti-treaty forces. In an RTE television programme in November 1997, it was suggested that he may have covered up the deliberate murder of eight Republican prisoners at Ballyseedy in 1922. He was Minister of Defense in 1923-1924 and Minister for Local Government in 1927. In the thirties he joined the Army Comrades Association which was formed to protect the Cumann na nGaedheal party meetings from attacks by the IRA. The organisation later became known as the Blueshirts, and was accused of having facist tendencies by its critics. Serious confrontation was avoided, however, and all parties opposed to Fianna Fail were encouraged, by Mulcahy and others, to join with Cumann na nGaedheal to form the Fine Gael party. His civil war and Blueshirt background precluded him from becoming leader of this party and the position was won by W. T. Costello. After the resignation of Costello in June 1944, Mulcahy became leader of Fine Gael. In the first coalition government of 1948 to 1951 he was Minister for Education and held the same ministry in the second coalition of 1954 to 1957. He resigned the leadership of the Fine Gael party in October 1959, and from the Dáil in 1961. He was a fluent Irish Speaker and Chairman of the Gaeltacht Commission of 1925-26. He died in Dublin on December 16th 1971.

MURPHY, DERVLA (b. 1931) of Lismore, Co. Waterford. Travel writer. Born in Lismore, the daughter of Fergus Murphy the County Waterford librarian. Educated locally and at the Ursuline Convent, Waterford. Published her first book, "Full Tilt: Ireland To India on a Bicycle" in 1965 and it was a huge success, being choosen as Book Society Alternative Choice for that year. In "A Place Apart" (1978) she wrote about Northern Ireland and won the Christopher Ewart - Biggs Memorial Prize. Other publications include; "Changing the Problem; Post-Forum Reflections" (1984), "Race to the Finish" (1981) about her horror at the nuclear arms race; "Tales from Two Cities" (1987), "Cameroon with Egbert" (1989), "Transylvania and Beyond" (1992), and "The Ukimwi Road" (1993). She has written sixteen books to date, including "South from the Limpopo : Travels through South Africa" (1997) A reviewer recently described her writing as ; "solid, chatty, unadorned and utterly reliable"(Sara Wheeler). Louis McRedmond's 20th Century Biographical Dictionary describes her as; "Unquestionably Ireland's best travel writer,.....her writing bursts with a love of humanity in it's myriad manifestations".

MURPHY, LIAM (b. 1948) Poet and storyteller. As a young poet in the sixties he held meetings of the Waterford Writers Workshop in his home in Rice Park where he encouraged other young writers including the late Sean Dunne to write poetry. According to Dunne, Murphy, "who had a reputation as a rebel", but at this stage was a published poet, once contributed a poem to a Christian Brothers' magazine in which he extolled the virtues of a former teaching brother. The magazine was widely circulated before it was discovered that the poem was an acrostic, and the first letters of each line contained a message which described the subject of the poem in the lowest possible terms. In later years Liam Murphy founded Cuala Verbal Arts which travels around the country from school to school demonstrating the art of story- telling. His publications include contributions to the Pan Anthology of Celtic Poetry and the Oxford Anthology of Irish Poetry edited by the late Sean Dunne.

MURPHY, NICHOLAS (NICKO) (b. 1947) Pioneering fisherman and co-op chairman. Born in Dunmore East, the eldest son of Joseph and Doreen (nee Strangman) Murphy. Nicko Murphy was educated at Killea National School and De La Salle College. After school Nicko went to sea and trained as a fisherman under the late John Roche, skipper/owner of the "Golden Feather". When in his early twenties he bought the ex-Scottish trawler "Wisemans". Dunmore East was historically famous as a port for herring boats, and perhaps for this reason the whitefish sector of the industry had been neglected. In 1974, Nicko Murphy - along with Trevor Simpson, Johnny Furlong, Brendan Glody, Maurice Glody, Len Clifford, Joseph Murphy and Ned Power were elected to the board of management of the newly formed Dunmore East Fishermen's Co-op Society Limited. In the early days the co-op relied on the fish landings of just a few old boats, including (apart from the "Wisemans") the "Accord" , skippered by the late Jack Doyle; the "Sure Swift", skippered by Patsy Downes, and the "Isle of Canna", skippered by Nicko's brother, John. [None of these boats, which had been built in the 'Forties, exist to-day. The "Wisemans" was sold and sank off Scotland. The "Isle of Canna" was broken up. The "Accord" was de-comissioned but refused to sink, and just floated away. The "Sure Swift", full of years and Toredo worms had to be broken up in the 1990s.] Nicko Murphy went on to acquire several new boats until at one time he had 5 boats fishing. Along with his brother Joseph, he was one of a handful of skippers who began fishing on the Porcupine Bank up to 100 miles west of Ireland. He made a number of exploratory trips for Bord Iascaigh Mhara, including several to the tuna and sword-fish grounds almost 300 miles south-west of Dunmore East. Towards the end of the Eighties he opened what has become a successful ship's chandlery business in Dunmore East. He has been chairman of Dunmore East Fishermen's Co-op Society Limited since 1974.

MURRAY, MILO and PAT, of Tourin, Cappoquin, Co. Waterford. These two members of the Cappoquin Rowing Club won five Gold Medals between them at the World Masters Rowing

Championships in Adelaide, Australia in 1997. Milo Murray is the well-known Waterford ICSMA County Secretary.

MULLANE, DERMOT (b. 1940) Broadcaster.
Although born in England, he spent his childhood in Waterford, where he and his family lived, initially at Thomas Street, and later at "Overgrange", Upper John's Hill. Educated at Newtown School and Trinity College (History & Political Science), he spent some years with *The Irish Times* before joining Telefís Eireann in 1972, where he became familiar to Irish viewers as the presenter of news and current affairs programmes. He later worked as a producer before taking up his present position as Executive Editor of Planning at RTE.

MUSGRAVE, SIR RICHARD Bart (1757-1818) of Tourin, Co. Waterford. Irish political writer. MP for Lismore 1778; created baronet, 1782; wrote on contemporary political events. Although he was in general a supporter of the English connection, he was opposed to the Act of Union.

MUSGRAVE, SIR RICHARD (1790-1859) Third baronet and nephew of the first baronet, was a liberal MP for Waterford. In 1826 he, along with Mr. O'Shea of Gardenmorris, proposed and seconded the nomination of Henry Villiers Stuart (q.v.), a supporter of Catholic Emancipation) as a candidate for the Parliamentary elections of that year, in opposition to Lord George Beresford. After the Famine he (along with some other landlords) was praised for his "exertions in relieving the destitution of the people" (*Cork Examiner* May 3rd 1847).

N

NAGLE, Mrs (fl. 1650s) A woman who greeted Cromwell outside Dungarvan with a jug of beer and thereby, legend has it, earned mercy for its defeated inhabitants.

NEWMAN, W. A. (ALEC) (1905-1972) Waterford -born journalist whose family moved to Belfast in 1912. He was educated at the Royal Belfast Academical Institute and at Trinity College, Dublin. In 1930, following a teaching post in Dublin, he joined *The Irish Times* and from then until 1961 held the posts, successively, of leader writer, assistant editor and editor. He then joined *The Irish Press* as a leader writer. He died in Dublin on March 6th 1972.

NEWPORT, SIR JOHN (1756-1843) A member of a prosperous and influential family in Waterford in the 18th Century. In 1792, when Sir Simon Newport was mayor, no less than three other Newports were aldermen, including Sir John (who was born in Waterford and educated at Eton and Trinity College, Dublin). He became a partner in his father's bank, which was then the most important financial institution in Waterford, and an officer in the Waterford Cavalry (Militia). In the 1780s he became an Alderman in Waterford Corporation, and after some years' service he was created a baronet. Following his marriage to Ellen Shapland Carew he unsuccessfully sought the Waterford seat in the general election of 1802, being defeated by William Congreve Alcock. However, he appealed to Parliament on the grounds that over one hundred freemen had been created on the day before the election to support the Alcock faction. He won his appeal and took the seat in December 1803. He retained this seat for the next 29 years with the support of Catholic and liberal Protestant voters. He died at his home in Newpark in 1843 and *The Waterford Mirror* of Feb. 10th that year reported that;

"In his parliamentary career Sir John was always a warm

and eloquent advocate of the Catholic Relief Bill and every
other measure that tended to the freedom and civilization
of mankind. In the House of Commons no opinion was
more looked to or had greater weight than Sir John
Newport's."
Sir John's brother William, who lived at Belmont in Ferrybank,
managed the family bank, which had helped to finance the
bridge over the Suir and other enterprises, including the
Catholic church at Carrick-on-Suir. In the recession of 1818-
1820, when a number of regional banks collapsed, Newport's
bank survived, but the stress imposed on William was such that
he committed suicide. It was said that William's doctor
hastened to the bank to withdraw his money. In any event the
subsequent run on the bank quickly brought about its collapse
in 1820, leading to widespread misery amongst ordinary savers
as well as the wealthy. (ref. T.G.Fewer)

Nic DHIARMADA, BRIONA (b.1957) Irish writer and academic.
Born in Waterford, she moved to Co. Wexford as a child. She was
educated at TCD and UCD and became an acknowledged
authority on the revival of Irish in the last century, as well as a
commentator on modern Irish literature. She gained a post as a
lecturer at UCD and has published amongst other works ; 'Ceist
na Teanga: Dioscursa na Gaelige'; 'An Fhiliocht agus Dioscursa
na mBan' (1982), 'Bláthu an Traidisiún' (1987), and 'Léirmheas
ar Cé hi sin Amuig ' (1993).

NOLAN, JIM (b. 1958) Playwright and Director. Born in
Waterford on June 11th 1958, he was educated at Mount Sion
CBS . His interest in theatre began, when, as a young lad of 15
or 16 he used to enjoy "the annual diet" of theatre provided for a
short while each year by the Irish Theatre Company at the
Theatre Royal, Waterford. Later while working at the Dublin
City Library, he spent much of his spare time attending the
theatre in Dublin. He returned to Waterford and began writing
and directing plays including "The Black Pool" in 1984. In 1985
he founded (with Ben Hennessy and Jim Daly) the Red Kettle
Theatre Company. The Company's first production was his "The
Gods are Angry Miss Kerr" (1985). In 1988 Red Kettle became
a professional company, coincidental with the opening of the

Garter Lane Theatre, which was to be (and still is) the venue for many of their productions (along with Waterford's Theatre Royal). The Company annually tours the principle theatrical venues of the country, including Dublin, Galway, Limerick and Cork as well as Belfast and Derry. Other plays written by Jim Nolan include "The Boathouse" (1986), "Dear Kenny" (1988) and he also wrote "Moonshine" (The Gallery Press, 1991) and "The Guernica Hotel" 1994. He received the OZ Whitehead Award in 1985, The *Sunday Independent* Theatre Award (1988), the RTE/Bank of Ireland Theatre Award (1992), and Jury's Achievement Award (1992). In January 1998 his play " The Salvage Shop" (which starred Niall Tobin, and was directed by Ben Barnes) premiered in the Garter Lane Theatre and received enormous praise. The three-week opening run was sold out within a few days. Liam Murphy, reviewing the play for The Munster Express, praised " some of the finest emotional scenes I have ever seen on a Waterford stage". Michael Browne of the same paper said he had rarely seen such a spontaneous standing ovation given to a play.

O

O'BRIEN, JAMES. Angler. Member of Waterford's Rinneshark Fishing Club, chosen to captain the Irish Sea Angling Team at the World Shore Angling Championships in Denmark in 1998.

O'BYRNE, CARMEL (1936-1994) Opera singer. Though born in Ennis, her family moved to Tramore when she was a child. Her father was an official with the National Bank in Waterford. She was sent to school at Laurel Hill in Limerick, and obtained a scholarship to University College, Galway, where she took a degree in languages. She started singing at the age of 8, and after college moved to Italy where she trained with the baritone, Gino Bechi at Palermo. Bechi immediately recognised that she had an unusual volume and extension of voice which gave her an equal capacity as a coloratura, lyric, and dramatic soprano. While in Italy, she met and married Dr Alfredo Ferlisi, a lawyer, and settled in Orvieto. She reached a high level of professional skill, touring and singing all over the world, from Belgrade to Argentina, and from Sydney to London. In 1966 she sang with the Dublin Grand Opera Society and the RTE Symphony Orchestra. She also sang in the Wexford Opera Festival. In 1986 a second tour of India had to be cancelled when she first became ill with cancer. However, for the next seven years she continued to sing whenever possible. She gave her last performance in the cancer ward of Orvieto Hospital for the benefit of her fellow patients. She died in Orvieto in 1994, and was buried at the Holy Cross Church, Tramore, on February 16th of that year. Her family still lives in Tramore.

O'CARROLL, FINTAN (1922-1981) Music teacher and composer. Born in Wexford in 1922. His father was from Kells, Co. Kilkenny and his mother was a Doyle from Ladies Island, Co. Wexford. His earliest recollection is of listening to the gramaphone, which was used to keep him quiet as a child, although he had an interest in music from an early age. The family moved to Waterford when he was nine, and he began playing musical instruments whenever he had a chance. He also tried his hand at composition, and won a competition at twelve years of age. Traditional music was his main interest and he competed successfully at Feiseanna, encouraged by his parents who sent him to music lessons whenever they could afford it. At 18 years of age he joined Great Southern Railways as a clerk. He studied with Miss Maud Redmond for three years and in 1944 became a pupil of Hermann Gebler. He made his debut as a violinist on Sept. 26th 1944, when he played Beethoven's Sonata No. 1 in D for Waterford Music Club, and in November of that year, had his first professional engagement as 2nd violin in "Maritana". In 1949 he became interested in choral and organ music and experimented with compositions for a mass. In that year he entered the Feis Ceoil in Dublin where he won the gold medal for viola and came 2nd in the Senior Violin. In the next few years he remained 'in the medals' but never won better than second in the Piano & Violin duet, a situation which irritated him extremely. He was offered the place of organist at the Dominican Church in Waterford in 1949 but left after 6 months. He married Josephine Kavanagh in 1952 and in the following year he founded the Waterford Orchestral Players. He imposed a severe disipline on his players and admitted "practices were long and ardous" but the result was a semi-professional orchestra which was always in demand in the south-east of the country for concerts, grand opera, etc. In 1958 he was asked to be musical director of the St. Patrick Brass Band and stayed with them until 1969. He also studied for and took a diploma in music from the NUI in 1967 and resigned from CIE in the same year to begin teaching full-time. He became choirmaster of the Friary and wrote "The Mass of Angels", and (in 1973) wrote the responsorial psalm (Psalm 22) "is é an Tiarna n'aoire". He subsequently became organist at St. Joseph & Benildus, and apart from many private students, he later returned to teach brass band instruments at his old school (Mount Sion). In the late seventies he wrote what he describes as "a very simple congregational mass, "Mass of the Immaculate Conception" which has since become widely used in Ireland and overseas. He also wrote some works for orchestra based on historical folk material, including - "Romance for Horn and Orchestra" and

"Three Irish Dances" both of which have been recorded by the RTE Concert Orchestra.

O'CONNOR, AINE, (1948-1998) Television presenter and journalist. Born in Waterford, the daughter of Liam and Betty O'Connor. Educated at the Ursuline Convent. Worked for RTE for a time as a presenter and journalist before becoming a producer. A close friend and business associate of the actor Gabriel Byrne, she was preparing to direct her first feature-length film, starring Byrne, when she died after a short illness.

O'CONNOR, JOHN (b.1952) Musician and journalist. Born in Parliament Street and raised in Ferrybank, Waterford, he was educated at Waterpark College and Ferrybank N.S. Although he has spent most of his working life to date as a journalist with the *"Munster Express"*, he spent several very active years as a sought-after musician during the showband era of the Sixties and Seventies. He played in London for some time before returning to Ireland to join the Dixies Showband with whom he had two Top Twenty hit records. He aso toured Canada with the Dixies. He returned to the *"Munster Express"* and established a first-class reputation as a journalist, and as a regional correspondent for RTE Radio and Television. His autobiographical book, "The Munster, The Music and The Village" was published in 1996.

O'CONNOR, PATRICK (b. 1943) Film director. Born at Ardmore, Co. Waterford, and educated at Christian Brothers Schools in Lismore and Cork. After emigrating to the USA he attended the University of California. Moving to Canada, he took a degree in cinema and video at the Ryerson Institute. He returned to Ireland and worked for RTE from 1971 to 1983, directing "The Ballroom of Romance" by William Trevor which earned him a BAFTA award and a New York Silver TV award. He also directed "Cal" (1984) and "A Month in the Country" (1987). He subsequently moved to Hollywood and directed "Circle of Friends" (1995) by Maeve Binchy, and "Inventing the Abbots" (1997) starring Joaquin Phoenix, Billy Crudup, Will Patton and Liv Tyler etc.

O'CONNOR, PETER. World Champion Long Jumper. Although born in Wicklow, he spent most of his life in Waterford. He commenced his athletic career in 1898. On September 17th 1899 he competed in his first All-Ireland Athletic Championship, and broke the world record for the long jump. At the same meeting he broke records in the 200 yards race and the Hop, Skip and Jump (48 feet). In 1900 he competed in twenty athletic meetings and won an incredible 37 first places, 13 seconds and 11 thirds. In Dublin in 1901 he set a world record in the long jump of 24 feet, 11.75 inches. This remained an international record for 25 years and an Irish record for 89 years. O'Connor was British Long-jump champion every year from 1901 to 1906. In the 1906 Olympics he won the Gold Medal in the Hop, Skip and Jump and the Silver in the long jump. At the time of course, Irish athletes competed under the British flag, but at the medal ceremony O'Connor refused to wear British colours and insisted on waving a green flag to indicate his nationality. This was regarded as being shocking 'bad form' at the time. His son, the late Peter O'Connor, practised as a solicitor in Waterford up to the nineteen-eighties. His grand-daughter, Hillary O'Connor, is a doctor in Dublin.

O'CONNOR, PETER (b.1912) Republican, socialist and anti-fascist. Resides at 9 Parnell Street, Waterford. Born at Keiloge, Waterford on March 31st 1912, but the family moved to 86 Poleberry in Waterford when he was aged one. He father and three brothers were all active trade unionists with a Republican background. He joined Fianna Éireann at the age of ten, and (in his own words) "was transferred" to the IRA at 17. As a young man in the hard times of the 1930s he played an active part in representing the unemployed and developed an abiding interest in socialism, helping to establish a Workers' Study Club where the writings of Connolly, Marx and Lenin could be studied and discussed. Resigning from the IRA he helped re-form the Communist Party of Ireland, and became involved in the socialist Republican Congress which met in Dublin in 1934. After the congress he and Billy Power of Waterpark Lodge, desperate to find work, stowed away on the *"Walnut"*, a small collier, berthed at the Scotch Quay in Waterford. During the rough crossing they were discovered, but treated kindly by the captain, who landed them at Newport, in Wales. (the *"Walnut"* foundered in a storm on it's next voyage, with the loss of all aboard). The two young men eventually got to London and found some work. Two years later, with 3 other Waterford men (Johnnie and Paddy Power and Jackie Hunt) he travelled to Spain and joined the International Brigade to fight fascism. From late February to the end of July 1937, he was involved in heavy fighting, particularly on the Jarama Front, and saw many of his comrades die. He almost died from typhoid on two occasions, because, as a teetotaller, he drank unpurified water instead of wine. In all, 19 Irishmen died on the Jarama Front in 1937, including Maurice Quinlan of South Parade, Waterford. O'Connor was sent home at the end of July. In 1938 he joined the Labour Party (but retained his membership in the Irish Communist Party) and was a member of Waterford Corporation for a few years in the 1950s. In 1994 he and his wife Biddy (neé Hartery, of Ballybricken) flew out to Spain for the unveiling of a monument commemorating the International Brigade at Jarama. In 1996 Peter O'Connor was made an honorary citizen of Spain.

O'DONOGHUE, FRANK (b. 1939) Chief executive, Waterford Chamber of Commerce. Born in Cork on Jan 12th 1939, the eldest son of Vincent O'Donoghue of the Munster & Leinster Bank. After his family moved to Waterford in 1947 he was educated at Waterpark College and the Institute of Personnel Management. Joining Allied Irish Banks, he became assistant manager at Waterford and Cork. In 1970-76 he served as regional development officer, IDA, Cork, and was personnel manager of Topps Ireland (Cork) in 1976-1980. He was personnel manager of Bausch and Lomb, Waterford from 1980-1997 before becoming chief executive of Waterford Chamber of Commerce. He has also represented Munster in tennis.

O'DONOGHUE, REDMOND (b.1943) Chief executive, Waterford Crystal. He was born in Waterford on March 12th 1943, the second son of Vincent O'Donoghue. He was educated at Waterpark College; University College, Dublin and Harvard Business School. Spent most of his business career with the Ford Motor Company in the U.K., Spain, and Ireland. In 1985 he joined Waterford Crystal as sales and marketing director. The company was at this time in a period of decline, and O'Donoghue was associated with, and (ultimately), directly behind, many of the developments which would return the company to its present high levels of profitability, including the acquisition of Wedgwood in November 1986; the launch of the company's first new brand, "Marquis by Waterford Crystal" in 1991; and what has been described as "the blistering pace" of the new product development programme. New products now account for 23 per cent of sales. In 1995 he was appointed chief executive and has since brought in John Rocha to add new designs to the glassware range and has successfully extended the "Waterford" brand beyond crystal into products such as Waterford Linen, Waterford China, Waterford Writing Instruments and Waterford Holiday Heirlooms. In 1997, Waterford Crystal increased sales by 21 per cent to £184.7 million and operating profits by 32 per cent to £23.7 million.

O'FÁINÍN, PADRAIG (b. 1918) Life president Mount Sion GAA. Born in Waterford on August 25th 1918, he was educated at Mount Sion CBS. He worked in the Department of Social Welfare from 1939 to 1983, and played for Mount Sion GAA Club for most of his sporting life, winning a Minor Hurling Medal in 1936 and seven county senior hurling championship medals between 1938 and 1949. He also played for Waterford. He was three times chairman of the GAA Waterford County Board (1955-1963, 1969-70, 1975-1987) and also served as president of the GAA Munster Council (1962-1965) and as president of the GAA (1970-1973). From 1940 to 1955 he was Hon. Secretary of Mount Sion GAA Club before becoming chairman (1955 to 1970 and 1977 to 1985) In the latter year he was elected club life president. In 1989 he became chairman of the board of management of Mount Sion Secondary School – the first layperson in Ireland to hold this position – until he retired in 1997.

O'FLAHERTY, STEPHEN (1902-1982) Entrepeneur, Born in Passage East, Co. Waterford. As a young man, he worked in England and at age of 25 he joined the Ford Motor Company in Cork. After the Second World War he moved to Dublin where he and his wife founded Motor Distributors Limited. The complete set of parts of a dozen Adler cars had been imported in crates before the war and had been gathering dust ever since. O'Flaherty bought them cheaply, assembled them and sold them at a considerable profit. This early sign of his abilities helped him to acquire the franchise (in 1949) for the distribution of Volkswagen cars in Ireland, and later, in Britain. He also acquired the franchise for the distribution of Merecedes-Benz.

O'FLAHERTY, KATHLEEN MARY, Academic and author, Born Co. Wexford. Educated at the Ursuline Convent, Waterford; the University of Lille, in Flanders, France; and UCC (where she took her Ph.D.) She served as assistant to the President of UCC from 1944 to 1952, while also lecturing in French language and literature. She was appointed Professor of French in 1970. Her area of specialised interest is Chateaubriand and her published works include; "The Novel in France" (1945), and, "Voltaire, Myth and Reality" (1945).

O hEOCHA, COLM (b.1926) President of University College Galway. Born Dungarvan, Co. Waterford, he was educated at Coláiste na Rinne; the Christian Brothers School, Dungarvan; Coláiste Iosagain, Baile Mhuirne, Co. Cork; UCG; and UCLA. O hEocha taught at UCLA in the 1950s and at the University of Minnesota in the early 1960s before being appointed professor of biochemistry at UCG (1963) where he became college president (1974-96). In 1983-84, he chaired the New Ireland Forum. He served as chairman of the Arts Council 1989.

O'KEEFE, PATRICK (1891-1938) Born in Waterford and lived at No. 2 Spring Garden Alley. As a young man he decided to emigrate to the United States and booked passage on the ill-fated White Star liner "Titanic", despite premonitions about the voyage. When the ship was sinking, O'Keefe jumped into the sea and found a collapsible raft, onto which he pulled several survivors, until eventually 20 people had been rescued. He was highly praised for his actions, but thereafter had a dread of sea journeys and never returned to Ireland.

O'KEEFE, THOMAS (b. 1929) Born and raised in Johnstown,

Waterford, he was educated at Waterpark College and the
Institute of Chartered Accountants. After marrying Gay
Fortune of Lower Newtown he emigrated to Brazil and joined
the Coca Cola Company. He later became president of Coca Cola
in Brazil and in due course president of the company for all of
South America. He is presently Brazilian Consul-General for
Ireland.

O'MEARA, MICHAEL. In 1927, Michael O'Meara established
the Waterford Beagles with the assistance of Denis Cleary, T. H.
Gallwey, Paddy O'Brien, Harry Sage, Willie Grant, Robin
Dawson, Nicholas Walton and others. Initially set up under the
patronage of the Catholic Young Men's Society, the revival of
beagling in Waterford was due to a large extent to the
encouragement of Michael O'Brien, the master of the Clonmel
Beagles, who supplied advice and seven hounds at 10 shillings
each. Previously, beagles had been hunted in the Tramore and
Waterford area by Mr. A. D. A. Bruce between 1900 and 1920.
In 1997 over 200 people attended a dinner at O'Shea's Hotel,
Tramore to celebrate the club's 70th birthday.

O'SHEA, BRIAN (b. 1944) Politician. Born in Waterford and
educated at Mount Sion CBS and St Patrick's Training College,
Dublin. He worked as a Primary school teacher in Tramore CBS
(1964-1970) and St. Pauls Boys NS, Waterford (1970-1987)
before taking his seat in the Senate in 1987. In 1989 he won a
seat in the Dáil as a member of the Labour Party and was re-
elected in 1992. He was appointed Minister of State (Food &
Horticulture) in 1993, which post he held until 1997, and in the
election of that year he was re-elected to the Dáil. He is a former
president of Waterford Council of Trade Unions and a Member
of Waterford County Council and Waterford City Council (1985 -
1993). A resident of Sweetbriar Lawn, Tramore, he was also a
member of Tramore Town Commissioners (1979-1993).

P

PALLISER, JOHN (1807-1887) Geographer and explorer who travelled in North America, in the unknown regions of the far west, between 1847 and 1861. Born at Comeragh House, Co. Waterford, John Palliser was the eldest son of Colonel Wray Palliser, a well-to-do Irish landowner and a descendent of William Palliser, a former Church of Ireland Bishop of Cashel. At the age of 38, having served as High Sheriff of the County, as well as JP and an officer in the Waterford Militia, he became restless and sailed to North America, travelling up the Mississipi to Independence, the gateway to a largely uncolonised "wild west". There he travelled with traders, lived and hunted bufallo with the Indians, shot grizzly bears and wolves, and had narrow escapes from hostile Indian war parties. He returned to Ireland, bringing three live buffalo and a pet wolf-dog to Comeragh House, where encouraged by his family, he wrote a book about his experiences called "Solitary Rambles and Adventures of a Hunter in the Prairies". It was an immediate success when published in 1853. In 1857, financed by the British Colonial Office and the Royal Geographical Society, he returned to North America in charge of an expedition whose task was to explore what is now western Canada. His party included a geologist, a botanist and an astronomical observer, and for three years they travelled up rivers an over enormously wide stretches of unpopulated prairie, mapping the area, finding passes through the mountains, and recording the flora and fauna (they collected thousands of specimens of plants, animals and insects). Their report was not published until 1862, and it was 1865 before a map was produced. Many of the names they put on geographical features are still in use today, such as the Palliser Pass, Palliser Range and the Palliser Triangle. The famous Kicking Horse Pass commemorates a serious injury sustained by James Hector, the geologist of the party, when kicked by his horse. The maps drawn by Palliser became the basis for the provinces of Alberta and Saskatchwan although it was in fact many years before the real value of his expedition was realised, and twenty years before he was acknowledged with a modest decoration (the CMG) by the Colonial Office. The Royal Geographical Society awarded him the Victoria Gold Medal and made him a Fellow of the Society. In 1960 the province of Saskatchewan celebrated the centenary of his expedition. John Palliser retired to Comeragh House, where, on the 12th of August, 1887, he died peacefully after a walk in the Comeragh Mountains. He is buried in the family tomb in Comeragh Churchyard. Comeragh House was severely damaged by fire on February 18th 1923, and much of John Palliser's records were destroyed. In more recent times it was the home of war-crimes suspect Peter Menton, who died while awaiting trial in Holland. On August 21st 1977, with considerable ceremony and accompanied by a military Guard of Honour, Mr. R.C. Pickering, Agent General of the Province of Alberta, unveiled a plaque to the memory of John Palliser at Briska Church. A wreath was laid by Mr. Wray Galloway of Annestown, a grand-nephew of the explorer. (ref. Irene M. Spry)

PALLISER, Sir WILLIAM (1830-1882) A soldier and inventor, he was a brother of John Palliser (q.v.) of Comeragh House. He was educated at Trinity College, Dublin and Trinity College, Cambridge, and invented numerous devices mainly to do with military projectiles. In 1862 he invented a method of converting smooth bores into rifled guns. In 1863 he produced a patent for chilled cast-iron shot, which for a time superseded steel projectiles. Chambers Encyclopaedia of 1882 reports: "The Palliser shell, which is now employed in the British service, is chiefly remarkable for the hardness imparted to its fire-point by a process of 'chilling' during casting. This gives it a great power of penetration into iron plates, etc.". William Palliser was knighted in 1873.

PARKINSON-HILL, CHARMIAN (see Hill, Charmian)

PARKINSON, JIM. Horse trainer of Tramore in the twenties, who trained two Irish Derby and four Oaks winners.

PARLE, Captain. Waterford Harbourmaster in 1878, and

founder member of Waterford Boat Club. The Parle name lived on in the Boat Club well into the 20th century with John, Bill and Nick Parle rowing successfully for the club both in Ireland and abroad.

PAUL, Col. PATRICK, Free State Army Officer. see Whelan, Pax.

PAUL, SIR ROBERT (d. 1956) 5th Baronet. Son of Sir William Joshua Paul, Justice of the Peace and Deputy Lieutenant of Waterford, he lived at Ballyglan, Woodstown. As a young man in the nineteen-twenties he had held an administrative position in the law courts with the grand title of Clerk of the Crown and Peace. He was also master of the Gaultier Hounds for a number of years up to 1930. His mother, the dowager Lady Paul lived in Cliff House, Dunmore East. This house was later bought by Willie Watt, and is now the Candlelight Hotel. The late Riocard Farrell remembered Sir Robert (in the 1920s) as an impressive figure dressed in a huge bearskin coat, in an open horse-drawn trap, trotting in to town from Woodstown on winter mornings. Years after he retired and well into old age he was a familiar figure at meets of the Waterford Hounds. He employed a large staff of maids, grooms and gardeners at Ballyglan House. In 1768 a Sir Joshua Paul became the centre of a row concerning the granting of the freedom of the city. A number of prominent citizens complained that the freedom of the city "had been conferred upon foreigners to the exclusion of those legally entitled to it." Sir Joshua Paul was one of those objected to on the grounds that he was lodging with his mother and therefore was not a bona fide (rate-paying) resident. When legal action was taken the court found in favour of the citizens. The records also show that in 1788 a Robert Paul, attorney at law, had an office on John's Hill, Waterford, while in the same decade a Captain Joseph Paul commanded the Waterford (Militia) Artillery (P. Power). The Pauls were related to the Carew family. When Sir Robert Paul died, Ballyglan House was taken over by Major Dennis Profumo, the brother of John Profumo, Conservative Minister of War who had to resign when the newspapers discovered that he had been having an affair with call-girl Christine Keeler (at the same time as Russian naval attache, Captain Ivanov). For a short while Ballyglan provided a refuge for the disgraced ex-minister. The property has changed hands several times since.

PEARE, WILLIAM F. (Bill) (1868-1948) One of Ireland's first motor dealers and assemblers, Bill Peare was born in Carrick-on-Suir in 1868. In 1895 he joined with W. (Billy) Merdith, a top racing cyclist, in setting up a cycle business. Three years later he imported a De Dion engined motor tricycle and in 1899 he built (from the components of this machine) a four-wheeled "car" which had it's first trial run on the Dunmore road. In 1900, Merdith left the company and William Goff became his partner in a new company, W.F. Peare Ltd, with a premises at Henrietta Street. The Peare Quad was advertised at this time as having a water cooled De Dion engine and a two speed gearbox. The first issue of the *The Irish Motor News* announced that the first car produced by Peare was sold to Captain H. Langrishe of Knocktopher Abbey, Co. Kilkenny. William Goff was the second customer to buy one of these cars. At this time, there were only about 50 cars in private hands in the whole country. In 1902 the company opened their "Motor Works" in Catherine Street, in what is believed to be the first 'garage' in Ireland. In 1903 Peare was appointed agent for Werner Motorcycles and in the same year formed the South-Eastern Branch of the Motorcycle Union of Ireland at the Imperial Hotel. In the years that followed he was agent for a number of car manufacturers, including Daimler, Oldsmobile, Gladiator, Vulcan, Delauney, Belleville, Napier, Buick, Cadillac and the famous Stanley Steam Cars. In 1908 he was charged with exceeding the speed limit at Callaghane Petty Sessions. In 1911 he applied for a licence to store petrol at the premises in Catherine Street, and two years later opened a branch garage in Cork. During the First World War Bill Peare, who was almost fifty, joined the Army. He attained the rank of captain and was mentioned in despatches. Unfortunately, a combination of his absence and wartime petrol rationing caused his company to go into liquidation in 1917. In the same year his wife died at the age of 37. After the war, Peare settled in England and did not return to Ireland until 1935, when he established another business in Dublin. He died in 1948 at the age of seventy-nine. In 1917 his motor works at

Catherine Street had been taken over by Waterford businessman John Kelly who re-opened the garage business in the same year. In 1928 John Kelly (Waterford) Ltd. was formed and has continued to trade under this name up to the present, currently under the management of David McCarthy, great-grandson of John Kelly.

PENROSE, GEORGE.   A Quaker merchant of Waterford city, who, with his nephew William, founded a glass factory in 1783, which was the predecessor of the now world-famous Waterford Crystal.   The Penrose factory opened for business at Merchant's Quay.   The Dublin Evening Post of October 4th 1783 carried the following advertisement: "George and William Penrose having established an extensive glass manufactory in this city, their friends and the public may be supplied with all kinds of plain and cut flint glass, useful and ornamental ; They hope that when the public know the low terms they will be supplied at, and consider the vast expense attending this weighty undertaking, they will not take offence at their selling for ready money only". Within three years over fifty craftsmen were employed.   In 1786, following a dispute, their leading craftsman, John Hill , an experienced glass-maker from Stourbridge, left the factory taking his recipe for the manufacture of crystal with him. Fortunately, he gave this secret to a fellow worker, Jonathan Gatchell, who used it to improve his position to a point where he eventually took over the firm from the Penroses.   The Penrose family was also involved in ship-building and in the latter part of the nineteenth century had a yard on the Suir near the flourmills.   William, Robert, Jacob and Henry Penrose at varying times advertised their ships for sale.

(O) PHELAN "Ó Faoláin (faol, wolf) One of the principle septs of the South-East.   Before the Norman invasion their chief was Prince of the Decies" (MacLysaght) "...an ancient tribe or family of the Decies..." (Canon Power) A political comentator called de Riva The O'Phelan lived on The Mall in 1934.

PHELAN JAMES. J. (fl. 1878) He was a founder member, in 1878, of Waterford Boat Club, along with Captain Parle, L.A. Ryan. A. Dillon, C. Ambrose, W. O'Donoghue, J. Locke and B.

Wright. The Club was fortunate in having in its early years an enthusiastic membership which went on to win most of the challenge cups in the south of Ireland. In their first year of competition they won their first races at the home regatta, beating Limerick Boat Club for the Waterford Challenge Cup, and Clonmel for the Suir Challenge Cup. The club made a point of being completely non-political and non-sectarian. Originally the club operated from a site on the South side of the river near Waterpark College but in 1885 a fine new clubhouse was built on the North side, just below the Abbey Church in Ferrybank. A leaflet issued by the club in the early part of this century describes it as follows;

> "Its premises which are picturesquely situated on the north bank of the river adjoin the public ferry and are easily accessible from it, while during the boating season a private ferry for member's use runs direct to the Club. The premises consist of a promenade, two landing slips, accessible at all stages of the tide, a large boat house with a reading room, dressing room, baths and lavatories, and a second house where teas and refreshments are served on regatta days and which is used as a store for boats during the winter".

In 1933, the Honorary Secretary, R.T. Poole, informed the membership that he had received a request for an Extraordinary General Meeting to consider the motion "That henceforth women shall be eligible for election to full membership of this Club". In 1936 the membership was informed by the then Secretary, G.E. Kelly, that membership had decreased to 118, that revenue from dances had disappeared , and that " Unless some means of increasing the Club's regular income can be devised......it will not be possible to carry on your Club much longer." In 1952 the Senior Eight won the Leander Grand cup, the Cork City Challenge Cup, the Shannon Rowing Club Challenge Cup, the Limerick City Challenge Cup and Laises Plate, the Devonshire Challenge Cup and Chearnley Challenge Cup (Cappoquin Regatta), the Urbs Intacta Challenge Cup, the Waterford Challenge Cup and the Suir Challenge Cup (Waterford Regatta) This super team consisted of E. Norris, R. Greer, S. Murphy, M. O'Hanlon, J. O'Meara, M. Flynn, W. McCarthy (Cox) D. Gaule (Stroke) and S. Sinnott. In 1963 a

Senior Eight crew from the Waterford Boat Club travelled to England where they competed with the top British , American and European Rowing clubs and won the Chester International Head of the River Race, one of the most sought-after trophies in rowing. The team, coached by D.J. Sinnott were; Andy Fitzgerald, Eddie Griffin, Tom Lonergan, Leo Murphy, Tony McCarthy, Frank Molloy , Tony O'Neill , P. Sinnott, and Terry Sinnott, cox. In 1978 Waterford Boat Club, to celebrate its centenary, held what was up to then , "the largest event ever staged on the River Suir, at which over 700 competitors in over 100 crews representing 28 clubs from the four provinces of Ireland, competed in 29 races." (*The Munster Express*). In the same year Killian O'Brien and Tony Corcoran of the Waterford Boat Club represented Ireland in Glasgow in the senior double sculls . In 1980 O'Brien and Corcoran won the Senior Championship. Killian O'Brien also represented Ireland in the European Championship (single sculls) in Switzerland and in the World Championships in Belgium. James J. Phelan's son, Frank Phelan, later served as President of the Boat Club for many years.

PHELAN, Dr JOHN (b. 1932) Medical doctor. Born in Waterford, he was educated at Waterpark College and University College Cork. He studied obstetrics in London and was Orthopaedic Registrar at St. Patricks before entering private practice in Waterford. As a general practictioner he went out of his way to bring modern thinking in medicine to his broad parish of patients. He was the principle founder, in 1988, of the Waterford Hospice Movement, which has become an essential and invaluable part of caring for the terminally ill in Waterford. The first formal meeting of the Waterford Hospice Movement took place in Ardkeen on the 13th of June,1988. Those in attendance were; Dr. John Phelan, (chairman), Mrs. Ita Shipsey, Ms. Maureen Sheedy, Mr. John Walsh, Ms. Marie Dennehy, Ms. May Lanigan, Ms. Noleen Deevy, and Dr. Chantelle McNamara.

PHELAN, JOHN (b.1962) of Bernard Place, Waterford. At the age of sixteen he won the All-Ireland Junior Squash Championship. Later he represented Ireland in numerous International Competitions and moved for a time to America where he became the U.S. National Squash Champion in 1988/89. He is almost unique in that he also represented the United States in international competition on five occasions. He is proprietor of the Reginald Bar and Restaurant, Waterford.

PHELAN, MARGARET - Ladies Gaelic Football player who was captain of the Waterford team which, on Sunday, October 12th, 1986, won the All-Ireland Ladies Football Final. It was the first time the ladies finals were held at Croke Park, and Waterford beat Wexford by the extraordinary score of 4-13 to 0-0. The other members of the team were; B. McGrath, B. Ryan, F. Wall, A. Fitzpatrick, N. O'Sullivan, D. Hallinan, M. Ryan, J. Whyte, M. Fitzpatrick, M. Crotty, C. Casey, U. McNamara, B. Ryan, and A. Meehan. Subs (who played) H. Walsh, C. Whyte and P. Butler. Also H. Condon, F. Fitzpatrick, D. Ryan, H. Walsh, A. Wall and S. Walsh. The scorers were; B. Ryan 1-5, M. Crotty 1-3, C. Casey 1-0, A. Meehan 1-0, U. McNamara 0-3, C. Whyte 0-1, and M. Ryan 0-1.

PHELAN, WILLIAM   Of Grantstown, Waterford, was the breeder of "Freebooter", Winner of the Aintree Grand National, 1950. " Freebooter" was by Steelpoint out of Proud Fury and was bought by English trainer Bobby Renton (it is said for £3500) for Mrs. Brotherton of Kirkham Abbey. In the race he was ridden by Waterford jockey Seamie Power. The race was a tough one. Out of 49 runners only 7 finished the course.

POCOCKE, DR. RICHARD (1704-1765) Bishop of Ossory (1756-1765). Born and raised in England and educated at Oxford, at the age of 20 his uncle, Thomas Milles, church of Ireland bishop of Waterford and Lismore, gave him the job of precentor at Lismore. From then on he rose steadily in the church, but managed to find the time to travel extensively not only in Europe but in Egypt, sometimes being away for several years at a time. He kept "journals" of his travels which he later published. In 1744 he was made precentor of Waterford, and in the following year, having dedicated one of these journals to Lord Chesterfield, the then Lord Lieutenant of Ireland, he was made archdeacon of Dublin. In 1756 the Duke of Devonshire (who succeeded Lord Chesterfield) made him bishop of Ossory.

During his time here he restored St. Canice's Cathedral in Kilkenny, badly damaged in the Cromwellian wars. In the last year of his life he was given the bishoprics of Elphin and Meath. He died on September 15th 1765 and is buried at Ardbraccan near Navan. John McVeagh describes Richard Pococke as "a man obsessed with travel. No less compulsive was his habit of writing every journey down." Although the journals of his continental travels were published in his lifetime, those of his Irish travels were not published until over 100 years after his death. They included: "Pococke's tour in Ireland in 1752" (Hodges, Figgis & Co, Dublin 1892) and "Pococke's Tour of South and South-West Ireland in 1758" (Journal of the Cork Historical and Archaeological Society 63 - 1958). In the former he describes Dungarvan as " a good fishing town, & famous for an export of potatoes to many parts of Ireland, & I have been told they export the yolks of eggs boyl'd hard & Salted for Spain to be eaten as sauce with their Salt fish; There is a bank about ten leagues from Dungarvan, where they catch great quantities of Hake & Haddock, Cod, Ling, & many other kinds of Fish. They have also a bed here of very large oysters..." (ref. J. McVeagh and Decies 42 - 1989)

POOLE. The name of a prominent family in Waterford in the 18th, 19th and early part of the 20th centuries. In 1788 a Richard Poole carried on business as a chandler and chemist in Patrick Street. Matthew Poole was a Magistrate, Surgeon, Physcian, Harbour Commissioner, Master of the Board of Guardians and Superintendent of the Fever Hospital in 1839. R. Poole & Co., Ltd., continued in business as Chemists and Druggists in 1896 and had premises at Michael Street and Lady Lane. Lily Poole was the second female ever to be elected to Waterford Corporation (just one month after Mary Strangman in 1912). R.T. Poole was an active member of Waterford Boat Club and was hon. secretary in 1933. But perhaps the greatest contribution, of a long-lasting nature, came from Poole's Photographic Studios, located at 134 the Quay at the turn of the century. They were responsible for an enormous amount of the photography taken in this area at the end of the last and the beginning of this century. Over 70,000 glass negatives survived and are now in the care of the National Library of Ireland. "This collection is the largest of it's kind in the country,...a unique resource for the people of Waterford and of Ireland". (D.Griffin)

POWER, ARTHUR (1891-1984) Artist and art critic, born in Guernsey and raised in Co. Waterford, he died in Dublin on May 7th 1984. Between the World Wars he lived in Paris where he started painting and became a friend of James Joyce. In 1922 he and Paul Henry put on an exhibition of "Modern Pictures" which featured a number of their friends from Paris including Modigliani and Maillol, as well as Cezanne, Matisse and Vlaminck. He is regarded as having played an important part in bring 'modernism' to Ireland. He was art critic for *The Irish Times* for several years and was a correspondent , while in Paris, for the *New York Herald*. In 1940 he wrote his first book, the autobiographical "From the Old Waterford House", and in 1974 published "Conversations with James Joyce". (ref. Louis McRedmond)

POWER, DAVID, of Duagh, in the Barony of Middlethird, Co. Waterford, was chairman of the Waterford Show Committee of 1990. This committee, which included Michael Hayes, Gilly Connors, Carmel Ryan, Maeve Phelan, Davie Sauvage, Dermot Ryan, Joe Widger, Francis Connors, Dixon Comerford, Phil Power, David Veale, Mick Connors, Caroline O'Donoghue, 'Statia Meade, Mickey Purcell, Noel Phelan, Harry O'Keefe, Carmel Flynn, Philip Murphy, Anna Jennings and Lena O'Connor, set out to re-establish the famous Waterford Agricultural and Equestrian Show of former years which became defunct in 1957. The original Show took place in a number of venues over the years including the Peoples Park and the football and greyhound stadium at Kilcohan. One of the earliest shows was held on the occasion of the opening of the Peoples Park in 1857, when manufacturers of agricultural implements from all over Europe were encouraged to come to the Park to show their wares by the then mayor, John A. Blake (1826-87) (q.v.) who worked like a Trojan to make it an outstanding show. Since its re-inauguaration, the present Waterford Show has grown from strength to strength and is currently regarded as the most important one-day show in the country. In 1990 the show was held at Ballinaneeshagh but since then it has been held at

Knockhouse, Gracedieu.

POWER, DERMOT (b.1947)   Local historian. Born and raised
at Doyle Street, Waterford, he was educated at Mount Sion CBS.
He started work in Waterford Glass in 1964 as an apprentice
glass cutter. In the 1970s he became an active trade-unionist,
representing the ATGWU. In 1982 he left to become a
professional musician and entertainer. Towards the end of the
1980s he became interested in local history, and in 1990 made
his first venture into writing, publishing two booklets on
traditional Waterford songs, many of which had never been
published in English before. There followed "The Street Where
You Live" (1992) and "Historic Anniversaries of Waterford City,
853 to 1994 " (1994). Since then he has contributed articles to
Decies, *The Munster Express*, and *Ireland's Own*. He has given
valuable service as a part-time curator of the Waterford Room in
the Waterford Municipal Library, and has lectured to the
Waterford Archaeological & Historical Society, the ICA, Probus
and other organisations.

POWER, EDWARD (b.1876) Professional diplomat. Born at
Ballyvoyle, Stradbally, Co. Waterford. He emigrated to the
United States, attended University and graduated with a degee
in law before becoming personal secretary and speechwriter to
Woodrow Wilson. Later he was appointed U.S. Consul in the
Phillipines, and Ambassador to Brazil. He also served as
Governor of the Panama Canal Zone.

POWER, FERGUS (1908-1997) Solicitor and Master of Beagles.
He was born at the Greenbank in Waterford city in May, 1908.
His parents were William and Margaret Power (nee Dooley).
His father was a butter merchant in the city but in 1912 he
bought a farm at Orchardstown, Butlerstown and moved the
family there.   His mother was a sister of Kate Dooley who
established Dooley's Hotel. Fergus was educated at Butlerstown
National School and at Waterpark College, and was then
apprenticed to James McCoy of Dobbyn & McCoy, where he
qualified as a solicitor in 1931. He remained with the firm for
the rest of his life and continued to practice up to his death, at
which time he was the oldest serving member of the Waterford

Law Society and one of the oldest practising solicitors in Ireland. He was highly regarded in his profession for his knowledge of the law and for his respect for it. He was an expert in fishery laws and successfully prosecuted many cases on behalf of the Southern Regional Fisheries Board. He had a vast knowledge of the townlands of County Waterford accumulated through his legal work and through many years walking the lands with gun or hounds. He was associated with the Waterford Beagle Club from its foundation in 1927, and was master and joint master from 1945 to 1984, and president from 1977 until his death. He was a founder member of the Irish Masters of Beagles Association and president and vice-president respectively of the association from 1976 to 1981, and 1982 to 1994. Hundreds of people will remember him as a tall, somewhat serious and determined-looking man, striding across the countryside in mud-spattered dark green coat and white breeches, preceeded by an eager pack of his beloved beagles. He had a deep love of the countryside and could 'read' it like a book. He loved hunting, which he took very seriously, and did not have much time for noisy followers who were unaware of hunting etiquette. In later years he mellowed somewhat, and always treated anyone who spoke to him with considered politeness. During the War (1939-45) he joined the L.D.F., which later became the F.C.A., and served with distinction for over 30 years, during which time he reached the rank of commandant, the highest rank possible for reserves. In 1947 he won a medal in the All-Ireland F.C.A. shooting competition. He was greatly disappointed when, at the age of 65, although fitter than most men twenty years younger, he had to retire. He had a dry sense of humour. On one occasion, when kennels needed repairs, and only poor scraps of timber were available, he was heard to murmer; "National motto - it'll do". In 1941 he married Mai Durkin. They moved to Tramore where they spent the rest of their lives. Mai died in 1991. Fergus had two sisters, Nora (Byrne) and Josephine. Josephine was married to his friend, the late Michael Morrisey, a well-known solicitor who practiced in Tramore and Cappoquin. Fergus and Mai had two sons, Bill and Ronan, and a daughter, Ann.

POWER, MICHAEL. Of Kill, Co, Waterford, was founding

huntsman and master of the Kill Harriers. The first meet of the Kill Harriers was at Kilbeg House on December 4th, 1977. For the next 20 years, 'Big Mike', as he was known to all, provided some of the best fox-hunting in the county. 'Good sportsmanship' could have been his motto, and this applied to the fox as well as the followers. As his name implies, he is a big man, and he always rode a large horse. In the course of a day's hunting he would cross railway embankments, rivers and stone walls, but he was never a fanatic and loved to see people having a good day out. In recent years his niece, Geraldine Power, accompanied him as whip. After the day's hunting, an equally good evening would be enjoyed in one of the pubs in Kill, where, on occasion, Big Mike would regale the company with a lively rendition of "The Shooting of Dangerous Dan McGrew" or one of his own compositions. Over the years the Kill Harriers became very popular, and the number of followers doubled. In 1997 he handed the huntsman's whip over to Gene Power, and took on a new joint master, Michael Feeney.

POWER, Very Rev. Canon PATRICK (1862-1951) Historian. He was born at Callaghane, three miles from Waterford city, in a thatched farmhouse (demolished in the 1970s) which was also said to have been a hiding place of Eamonn De Valera when he was on the run during the Troubles. Patrick Power was educated at Ballygunner National School, the Catholic University School, Waterford, and St. John's College. He was ordained in 1885 and spent three years in Liverpool before a threat of tuberculosis caused him to move to New South Wales in Australia. After seven years he returned to Waterford and was attached to the Cathedral for three years before becoming, successively, diosesan inspector of schools, chaplain to De La Salle Training College, and curate at Portlaw. He appears to have developed an interest in archaelogy while in Australia, and when he returned to Ireland this became a passion which started with ecclesiastical antiquities and then moved on to local history, place-names and local archaeology. For many years he was editor of the Journal of the Waterford and South East Ireland Archaeological Society. He wrote many articles and books, and having lectured in archaeology at Maynooth, became Professor of Archaeology at UCC in 1915. The National

University of Ireland awarded him the degree of D.Litt. in 1926. He continued to study and write to the end of his life. The work for which he is probably best known is his "Place-Names of the Decies" which was first published in book form in 1907, and was republished by the Cork University Press in 1952. His other publications include: "A Short History of County Waterford" (1933), "Waterford and Lismore: A Compendious History of the United Dioceses" (1937), "The Cathedral Parish of Holy Trinity, Waterford" (1940), and "St John's and Ballygunner" (1942). He died in 1951 and was buried in St. Otteran's graveyard, Ballynaneasagh.

POWER, ROGER (1921-1997) Farmer and local historian. Born and raised at Ballygunnermore, Waterford, Roger Power, in looks and in disposition could have inspired the phrase "one of nature's gentlemen". Although he never had a formal education in the subject, Roger had a life-long interest in local history and was the producer of "Historical Gleanings" for the "Waterford Today" newspaper. He was also an excellent 'dowser', or water diviner, and gave his services free to friends and neighbours over a wide area.

POWER, WILLIAM GRATTAN TYRONE (1797-1841) Actor. Born at Kilmacthomas Co. Waterford. His father died when he was a child and his mother moved to Cardiff. At fourteen years of age he joined a travelling theatre company and spent the next few years learning his trade as an actor. He was almost thirty before he made a name for himself as an Irish comic actor, under the name of Tyrone Power, and became a star at Covent Garden Theatre in London, after which he was in great demand, not only in many of the London theatres but also in Dublin. This was followed by several successful tours in America between 1833 and 1840. Unfortunately, on his last trip he choose to return on one of the early trans-Atlantic steamers, the paddle-steamer "President ". She sailed from New York on March 11th 1841, and was never seen again. Tyrone Power, the famous film star (1913-1958) was his great-grandson.

PURCELL, Sir HUGH (d. 1241) Founder of Fransiscan Friary Waterford.

PYNE, JASPER DOUGLAS, M.P. (1847-1888) At Lisfinn, near Lismore, stands the ruin of a sixteenth century Desmond castle or tower house which was the scene, in 1888, of a "half ludicrous, half-serious incident" of the Land Agitation of the late 19th Century.   In 1885, Jasper Douglas Pyne, who had inherited the castle, was elected MP for West Waterford of the Home Rule ticket. He had defeated Sir Richard Keane Bart. and in the general election of the following year was returned unopposed.   He was involved with the extremist side of the Nationalist-Land League movement and became identified as a "troublemaker" with the police. In October 1887, when William Shanahan of Scrahan was threatened with eviction by the Marquis of Waterford, Jasper Pyne encouraged him and his supporters to resist the Sheriff. Pyne then received intelligence that he was to be arrested by the police on a charge of incitement and immediately stocked the tower with provisions and barracaded himself inside. The police arrived but found the tower too great an obstacle. A state of siege existed for several months after which, under cover of a diversion on one side of the tower, Pyne escaped down a rope on the other side and fled to England. He was arrested outside the House of Commons three weeks later and returned to Kilmacthomas for trial. Although he was cheered as a hero by the people of county Waterford, he eventually had to serve 6 weeks in jail. Only a few months later he disappeared , presumably drowned, while crossing the Irish Sea on the ferry.

Q

QUAN. The name of a prominent merchant family in Waterford in the eighteenth and nineteenth centuries. The mother of Thomas Francis Meagher was a Quan, and her brothers Thomas and James were merchants and executors of James Wyse's will. A Thomas Quan was also a prominent shareholder in the company formed to build the bridge over the Suir in 1790.

QUINLAN, JAMES (1762-1826) Surgeon. He was born in Manganstown, Kilsheelan, Co. Waterford, a member of a prominent Catholic landed family. As a young man he fled to France to avoid the authorities who suspected he was involved in the 1798 Uprising. Under the patronage of an uncle he studied medicine at Louvain University . On qualifying he became a surgeon in the French army, but was wounded and captured by the Russians during the retreat from Moscow. However, his medical skills brought him to the attention of the Czar, who gave him his freedom and an important position in the medical heirarchy of Russia. He went on to become the Czar's personal physician, and Chief Surgeon in the Royal Hospital, Moscow. His descendants live at "Nirevale", in the parish of Four-Mile-Water. (M.Hallinan)

R

REDMOND, JOHN EDWARD (1856-1918). Political Leader. John Redmond was born in Co. Wexford in September 1856, the eldest son of William Redmond, MP for Wexford. Educated at Clongowes Wood College and Trinity College Dublin, he worked for a time as a clerk in the House of Commons before being called to the Irish Bar in 1886. He was a keen follower of Parnell, and was to support him to the end of his (Parnell's) life. In the years following his election as MP for New Ross, Co. Wexford, he undertook a successful fundraising tour of Australia and the United States. In 1890 the Irish Parliamentary party was split over the O'Shea divorce case and Redmond led the minority which supported Parnell. In 1891 he was elected MP for Waterford and held the seat until his death. In a speech at the St. Patrick's Day banquet in London in 1890 he said; "During this century the population of our country has fallen from eight and a half millions in 1841 to four and a half millions to-day. While every nation in Europe has advanced this century in prosperity, Ireland, under the deadly blight of British rule, has sunk, decade by decade, lower and lower in poverty. The industries of Ireland, with the single exception of the industry of agriculture, might be said to have absolutely disappeared, and every year the area of land going out of cultivation increased".

In the same year (1890), the Irish Parliamentary party became re-united under his leadership. Over the next few years he was vigorously involved in the Land Conference which led to the Land Act of 1903 (which offered a bonus to landlords to sell their lands and enabled tenants to purchase the lands on easy terms of sixty-eight years repayments), and the complex and detailed negotiations which led, finally, to the establishment, in 1908, of the National University. Redmond's ultimate objective was a form of independence within the United Kingdom, i.e., Home Rule. When the Liberal party came to power in 1906 Redmond decided to give his support to some of their objectives in the hope that they would support his. Thus, with the support of the Irish Parliamentary party, the Liberals, in 1911, carried through an Act which ended the veto of the House of Lords over the House of Commons. In 1912 the third Home Rule Bill was introduced, but was vehemently opposed by the Protestant population of Ulster, 200,000 of whom, led by Sir Edward Carson and many prominent churchmen and politicians, signed a Solemn Covenant to defeat it. When the Ulster Covenanters began to arm and drill, the Irish National Volunteers were organised by Eoin O'Neill, Pearse and others who no longer believed in constitutional reform. The Home Rule Bill was delayed by the House of Lords (who could still delay Bills for two years) and the outbreak of the First World War meant that, although it had received royal assent, it would not be put into effect until the war was over. Redmond appealed for volunteers to fight the Germans, and thousands joined up, including his younger brother William who was to die in action. In 1917 Redmond called for a national convention to draft a constitution for Ireland within the British Empire, but it had made little progress when he was suddenly taken ill and died on March 6th., 1918. He is buried in the family vault in St. John's Graveyard, John Street, Wexford.

REGINALD Mac IVOR, Danish chieftain of Waterford in 1003, he is credited with building Reginald's Tower (sometimes, down through history, referred to as Dondory, Reynold's Tower, or the Ring Tower). In fact, most historians and archaeologists agree that the tower as we know it to-day, is not the original tower, but one probably built on the remains of Reginald's fortification, perhaps in the 12th or 13th Century. It is believed to have been held as a fortress by Strongbow, Earl of Pembroke in the 12th Century, and used as a Royal Mint by statute from Edward IV in the 15th Century. In the Seventeenth and early Eighteenth century its cannons stood guard on the river. Approximately eight cannon formed a battery at the base of the tower, while long barrelled brass cannon of lighter bore bristled from the battlements. Since then it has been used as a prison; as a residence for the High Constable at the end of the 19th and beginning of the 20th century; as an air-raid shelter in World War Two , and in recent decades as a museum. Whatever about it's exact date of birth, it is thought to be the oldest public building in continual use in Ireland.

REYNOLDS, HARRY ; A member of the Waterford Bicycle Club who raced regularly on the Goff Track and was the first Irishman to win the World Cycling Championship (at Amsterdam in 1896). (ref. Muiris O'Ceallaig)

REYNOLDS, LAWRENCE (1803-1887) Medical doctor, soldier, poet. Born in Waterford, he studied medicine in England and started a practice in Liverpool. In 1862 he moved to New York and joined the 63rd Regiment of the New York Volunteers (Irish Brigade), and served throughout the American Civil War looking after the wounded at the front. He wrote a number of poems and songs in praise of the men of the Irish Brigade. After the war, he returned to the practice of medicine in Brooklyn, New York. Towards the end of his life he moved to Oswego, New York State, where he died on April 28th 1887.

RICE, EDMUND IGNATIUS (1762-1844) Founder of the Irish Christian Brothers. Born on June 1st 1762 at Westcourt, near Callan, Co. Kilkenny. He was educated partly at home and partly at a local hedge school. In 1778 he was apprenticed to his uncle in Waterford who was a prosperous merchant. The uncle died in 1790 and left the business to Edmund. Edmund had married in 1785 but his wife died after only four years (apparently in a riding accident), and left him with a handicapped daughter. This was the turning point in his life, and he decided to retire from business and devote himself to a religious life. With the support of the bishop, he founded a school for poor boys in the city in 1803, and soon had schools in other nearby towns, run by men who were equally devoted to Christian principles. On September 5th 1820 Pope Pius VII gave his official approval to this new congregation which he referred to as "the Institute of the Brothers of the Christian Schools of Ireland". Edmund Rice became Brother Ignatius and the first superior-general of the order. Among his friends and supporters were Daniel O'Connell, Charles Bianconi and Father Theobald Matthew. When he died in Waterford on August 29th, 1844, the Irish Christian Brothers had 22 schools spread over Ireland and England. He was beatified by Pope John Paul 11 on October 6th, 1996.

RICE, JAMES A popular mayor of Waterford in the 15th
century, he is remembered to-day for the macabre tomb he had
designed for himself which can still be seen in Christchurch
Cathedral. Carved in limestone, the tomb depicts a life-size
figure of a skeleton with worms crawling between his bones and
ribs, and a frog sitting where his stomach would have been ! The
epitaph reads;

"I am now what you will become,
I once was what you are now".

RICHARDSON, J. LIONEL (fl. 1940) Horticulturist who lived
at Prospect House, Waterford, and was famous for his work of
producing (in the Thirties, Forties and Fifties) new varieties of
daffodils. He won numerous prizes at the Royal Horticultural
Show in London over a number of years including the RHS Gold
Medal in 1940.

ROACH , JOHN (HAL) (b.1927) Comedian. Born in Waterford,
where he attended St. Declan's School. At the age of eleven he
won a talent competition at the Theatre Royal which resulted in
a trip to New Zealand. His likeness to producer Hal Roche's
character "Alphalfa" in the black and white movie series "Our
Gang" caused him to be nicknamed Hal. He returned to Ireland
and won another talent competition, this time on the Harry
Baily show, and from then on was well on the way to a career as
a top rank international comedian both at home and abroad.
Over the next thirty years, half the year was spent travelling
and the other half as top billing at Jury's Hotel Cabaret, in
Dublin. He is married with four children, one of whom, his only
son John, was born with Downes Syndrome. He has given much
of his time and money to establish "The Hal Roach School for
exceptional children" inspired by John.

ROBERTS,   FIELD-MARSHALL   LORD   ROBERTS   OF
WATERFORD AND KANDAHAR (1832-1914) Frederick Sleigh
Roberts was born at Cawnpore, India, September 30th, 1832,
first child of Lt.-Colonel (later General) Abraham Roberts by his
second wife. The Roberts family had been established in
Waterford for several generations and many had led
distinguished careers in the Navy, Army and the Arts. He was

the great-grandson of John Roberts,(q.v.) architect, who died in
1794. His father, Abraham, was born in Waterford in 1784,
joining the Waterford militia at a young age. Abraham's military
career progressed until at the time of Frederick's birth at
Cawnpore, India, he commanded a regiment. Frederick was
sent to Eaton at the age of thirteen, and a year later (1847), was
accepted at Sandhurst Military Academy (although he had lost
the sight of his right eye in a childhood illness in India). After
two years he transferred to Addiscombe, the East India
Company's military college. He joined the Bengal Artillery in
1851, and served with distinction during the Indian Mutiny,
(1857-58), winning the Victoria Cross. He returned to Waterford
in June 1858, on fifteen months leave. There he hunted with the
Waterford Hounds and met and courted Nora Henrietta Bews,
who lived at 'Landscape' on Passage Road. They were married in
Waterford on May 17th, 1859. They returned to India, where
Roberts spent a total of 41 years, gradually rising in rank and
responsibilities. Although originally an artillery officer,
opportunities arose for him as an assistant quartermaster-
general with Sir Robert Napier. The period, the climate, and the
vast theatre of operations in the East made logistics the key
factor in determining whether an army died in a desert due to a
lack of transport, ammunition, food or water; or marched home
weary but victorious. Immense and meticulous planning was
required, and this laid the foundation for Roberts's future
successes as a general. He had his first experience of the
demands of this job, when, at the age of 27, with the new rank
of major, he was selected to be in charge of the caravan of the
Governor General, who had decided to tour the Punjab and
North-West Provinces;

> "It was a mammoth task. With the Viceroy were to be not
> only his retinue, bodyguard and guests, but also the
> Commander-in-Chief, with his headquarters staff and
> escort. In all, tents for 20,000 persons were required. So
> Roberts went to Allahabad to get them out of store, where
> he found that a large number had deteriorated. They then
> had to be repaired, and the entire camp and its equipment
> arranged in duplicate so that the party could arrive and
> find everything as they had left it that morning. A
> 'village' was laid out daily on the same plan, with street

lamps, lanes and bazaars in the same relative positions.
Tradesmen's shops were provided for sweetmeat-men,
spice-sellers, grocers, fishmongers, a pawnbroker,
tobacconist, cobbler, egg and fowl merchant, tailor, baker,
and three butchers. There was also a post and telegraph
office. It was the duty of the local police to set up a station
in their alloted space, and forty roadmen were taken to
water the streets and keep down dust."

("Roberts" by David James)

By 1878 he was the Quartermaster-General of the whole Indian
Army. In the same year he was made a major-general and had
his first of several victories over the Afghans and captured
Kabul. In 1880 he made his celebrated march from Kabul to
Kandahar (10,000 men, with their supplies and baggage,
marched 320 miles over rough terrain in 21 days – the
temperature was 110 degrees Farenheit) resulting in the
'pacification' of Afghanistan, and preventing it from falling into
the hands of the Russians. Over the next twelve years honours
continued to accumulate, and when he left India in 1892 , he had
been made, successively, a knight, a baronet, and a baron. In
1895 he was promoted to Field-Marshal and commander-in-chief
in Ireland. This should have been a happy prelude to retirement
but in 1899, at the age of 67, he was called to London and was
asked to take command of the British Army, at a standstill in the
Boer War. Almost in the same hour, he received news of the
death of his only son Freddy, in action in South Africa (in a
dashing attempt to rescue artillery which earned him a
posthumous VC). There was no time to grieve, or reflect on the
almost unique fact that his son had won the same high award for
gallantry that he had won forty-one years before. Within two
hours he was on the boat-train to Dublin to pack his bags and
collect his war staff. On arrival in South Africa, he increased
the number of cavalry and improved the transport system, and
went on to defeat the Boers. For this he was made an earl and
Knight of the Garter. From 1900 to 1905 he was commander-
in -chief of the British Army. In 1914 an Indian Expeditionary
Force was sent to France to fight the Germans. Roberts was
given the largely honorary rank of Colonel-in-Chief.
Nevertheless, he went to visit them in France, caught a chill,

and died near St. Omer. He was 82. Although his name is no longer familiar to most people, he was an extraordinary man. He had suffered from serious illness as a child, he had impaired vision and was less than 5ft 5inches in height, yet he was possibly the most decorated soldier in the British Army. Apart from the Victoria Cross and other medals, he was Mentioned in Despatches on no less than 23 occasions. He was known as "Bobs" or "Little Bobs" to both his fellow officers and his men, who would have followed him anywhere. He was given the Freedom of the City of Waterford in 1893. After his death Rudyard Kipling wrote of him:

> *"Clean, simple, valiant, well-beloved,*
> *Flawless in faith and fame,*
> *Whom neither ease nor honors moved,*
> *An hair's breadth from his aim."*

ROBERTS, JOHN (1716-1796) Architect and builder. Born in Waterford, the son of a carpenter and builder who in turn was the son of a Welsh businessman. John grew up in Waterford, but may have been partially educated in London. At the age of seventeen he married Mary Sautelle, the daughter of a Waterford Huguenot family. In his career Roberts was involved in the design and building of many houses in Waterford. He built what is now Newtown School in 1786 as a residence for Thomas Wyse, and the City Hall in 1788. He built the forecourt at Curraghmore for the Marquis of Waterford between 1742 and 1750. He also built, as a private residence for William Morris, what is now known as the Chamber of Commerce building. His best-known buildings are the Protestant Christ Church Cathedral, and the Catholic Cathedral of the Most Holy Trinity. The former (completed in 1779) has been described by the English architectural writer, Marc Girouard, as "The finest 18th century ecclesiastical building in Ireland". The latter, started in 1793, is the oldest Catholic cathedral in Ireland. It is completely different in design from the Protestant cathedral, yet Girouard comments that, whereas "the Protestant cathedral is cool and northern, redolent of lawn sleeves and the communion service; the Catholic cathedral, with it's forest of huge Corinthian columns, is warm, luscious and Mediterranean". This was to be Roberts last work. A popular tradition in Waterford says that he caught a chill while waiting for workers, having arrived (apparently by mistake) at the draughty, unfinished building at three in the morning instead of six. He fell asleep and caught pneumonia from which he never recovered. He was eighty years of age.

ROBERTS, THOMAS (1749-1778) Painter. Son of John Roberts (q.v.). He is generally regarded as being a superior painter to his younger brother (Thomas Sautelle), and received commissions from wealthy and influential patrons, including the Duke of Leinster and Lord Powerscourt. He died when he was barely thirty, and thus has left only a small legacy of paintings behind.

ROBERTS, THOMAS SAUTELLE (1760-1826) Painter . Son of the Waterford architect, John Roberts (q.v.), and younger brother of Thomas Roberts (q.v.) also a painter (their mother was a Sautelle). On leaving school he was apprenticed to Dublin architect Thomas Ivory but preferred to paint and left Ivory for the Dublin Society Schools where he studied for several years before embarking on a career as a landscape artist, painting numerous scenes around Dublin and Wicklow. "He was subject to the emotional forces of Romanticism, and his landscapes in the early years of the nineteenth century display that love for the dramatic that was to become an important thread in Irish, as in English, painting through the century." (Arnold) He spent some years in London in the 1790s and exhibited at the Royal Academy. He returned to Dublin in 1799 but continued to send paintings to London for exhibition at the Royal Academy and the British Institution. He produced a number of paintings of Waterford City and county, including one of Curraghmore House, Portlaw, the forecourt of which had been built by his father, John Roberts in the 1740s. He was a founder member of the Royal Hibernian Academy and exhibited at their first exhibition at Abbey Street in 1826. Unfortunately, in the same year he injured his shoulder which prevented him from painting. He became deeply depressed and committed suicide at his house at Portobello. "His work, although of a high quality, was somewhat overshadowed by that of his more talented brother, Thomas Roberts (1748-1778). The influence of his brother's style can be seen in much of his earlier work."(Gillespie, Mooney, Ryan).

ROCHE, Colonel JAMES (fl. 1689) Nicknamed "The Swimmer" Roche. As an officer in the Williamite army during the siege of Derry, he swam up the river Foyle to tell the starving occupants to hold on as relief was on the way. As a reward for his bravery, King William gave him the rights to a number of ferry crossings throughout Ireland, including several on the River Suir at Waterford. However, many of these rights were hotly disputed, and Roche successfully appealed to the Crown for permission to exchange them for the forfeited estate of James Everard in County Waterford. Colonel Roche is buried at Castletown graveyard.

ROCHE, REGINA MARY (nee Dalton) (1764-1845) Novelist. Born and educated in Waterford, she published 16 novels between 1793 and 1834, including the popular, "Children of the Abbey" (1797). She lived for a time on the Mall in Waterford where she died on May 17th , 1845.

ROCHE, SAMPSON TOWGOOD, County Waterford artist of the early 19th century. He is considered to be one of Irelands finest miniaturists.

ROGERS, STEPHEN (b.1932) City councillor and Mayor of Waterford. Educated at Mount Sion CBS and the Central Technical Institute, he spent most of his working life in the Motor industry and as a young man was a keen supporter and follower of motor sport, especially rallying and hill-climbing. In the seventies he became involved in local politics and in 1974 was elected to the city council where he has been returned at each election since, originally on the Fine Gael ticket but since 1979 as an independent. He was Mayor of Waterford in 1979-80, when the borough boundries were extended, and again in 1994-95. A Peace Commissioner, he is a life member of Waterpark Rugby Club and Waterford Motor Club. He was married to the late Kathleen Doyle. They had one son, David, who died as a young boy in tragic circumstances. Stephen Rogers lives at Viewmount, Waterford.

RYLAND, RICHARD HOPKINS, Rev. (d. 1868) A member of a middle-class Dungarvan family which contributed many of it's members to the Church of Ireland clergy. He was an amateur historian and in 1824 published " The History, Topography and Antiquities of the County and City of Waterford", to correct what he described as "the incorrect ideas and false representations of flying travellers and tourists....." One of his six sons was precentor of Waterford diocese from 1864 to 1897, another, Theodore, was a barrister in Dublin. (ref.H.F.Morris)

S

SHALLOE, MICHAEL EDWARD. Waterford bicycle racing enthusiast and captain (in 1895) of the Waterford Bicycle Club, who broke a number of Irish records and had a cycle shop (The Cycle Depot) on the Quay in the 1890s. His son, Jack Shalloe, was a well-liked Chief Fire Officer of Waterford City in the nineteen-forties and fifties. (ref; Muiris O'Ceallaig)

SHEA, MATTHEW, (d. 1844) Tobacconist and vintner who had a shop in Broadstreet at the beginning of the 19th century. He provided in his will for a home for old people, to be called The Matthew Shea Charity. For a number of years there was a dispute over the use of these funds, and it was largely through the efforts of councillor John Blake, MP (q.v.) and John O'Brien, Town Clerk, that Matthew Shea's wishes were carried out, firstly at John's Avenue, and then some years later with the erection of a substantial building at the corner of the Manor and Bath Street.

SHEEHAN, Very Rev. Dr. Bishop of Waterford and founder (in 1894) of " The Waterford & South East of Ireland Archaeological Society".

SHERIDAN, MICHAEL P. (b. 1941) Public auditor and master of beagles. Born in Waterford, educated at Waterpark College and Castleknock College, Dublin. Trained in accountancy at Chambers, Halley & Co. Appointed public auditor by minister for finance. Member of Waterford Beagles since 1959. Master and joint-master since 1981. Lives in Tramore.

SHERIDAN, THOMAS J. (1887-1957) Businessman. Born in Co. Meath, he trained as a mechanic there and in Co. Cork, and at the age of 26 arrived in Waterford ("with nothing but the boots on my feet"). He started a bicycle shop, and then moved into the newly developing motor business. He was one of the first in the country to obtain an agency for Ford Motor Cars, and opened a garage at The Quay, Waterford in 1916. In later life he recalled how difficult it was to run his business during the Troubles, when both sides would call at his premises, put a gun on the counter, and "commandeer" a car. His solution to this problem was to keep only "bangers" in the showroom, while genuine buyers would be brought to his secret showroom in Marble lane. The business prospered and in the early Twenties he introduced Ford lorries. One morning he had to face an angry demonstration from barge men who feared their livelihoods would be taken away from them by the new lorries. In the 1930s he overcame a law preventing the import from England of fully assembled cars by cutting them in half, importing them, and then "re-assembling" them. By the outbreak of the Second World War he owned two garages in London, and one in in Middle Abbey Street, Dublin. After the war, he bought several thousand ex-RAF bicycles at a bargain price. A team of mechanics stripped them, sprayed the frames and re-assembled them with new parts. The re-modelled bicycles sold for about four pounds ten shillings and gave great service to thousands in the south-east for many years. In the 1950s he handed over the motor business to his son, and devoted his time to fishing for salmon and converting old houses into flats. While staying in the Clarence Hotel in Dublin in February 1957 he caught pneumonia and died in hospital a few days later. Sheridan's Motor Garage continues to prosper under the management of his great-grandson.

SHIEL, RICHARD LALOR (1791-1851)   Born at Bellevue, on the Kilkenny side of the river Suir on August 16th 1791. His father, Edward Shiel, had made a fortune trading into the Spanish port of Cadiz. His mother was a daughter of Count McCarthy of Toulouse, an Irishman who had sold up and moved to France to avoid the penal laws. Richard Shiel was educated at a private school in Kensington; Stonyhurst, Lancashire; Trinity College, Dublin; and Lincoln's Inn, London before returning to Ireland in 1813. To help finance the building up of his law practice he wrote and produced plays. He became one of the leaders of the Catholic Emancipation Movement and for a time, of the early Repeal movement, but according to Arthur Griffith he abandoned it (describing it as "a splendid phantom") in exchange for positions offered to him by the British Government. He was appointed H. M. Plenipotentiary to the Court of Tuscany in 1851, but in the same year died, from an attack of gout, while in Florence.

SMITH, CHARLES, of Dungarvan, Co. Waterford. Apothecary and historian. Wrote "The Ancient and Present state of the County and City of Waterford" 1746. (see Decies 1997)

SMITH, SUSAN World class hurdler. Born in Waterford and educated at the Presentation Secondary School. At the 1997 World Championships in Athens, Susan Smith broke the Irish 400 metres record for the seventh time when she finished seventh in the finals of this event. Her time of 54.61 in Heat 3 of the 400 metres hurdles knocked just under 2 seconds off the old Irish record held by Mary Appleby. At the end of the Championships Susan ranked 2nd in Europe and 8th in the world.

STANHOPE, ARTHUR Rev. (d. 1685) Clergyman and writer. In 1670 he was appointed Vicar-General of Waterford and Lismore, having served as Church of Ireland vicar in a number of parishes in the diocese, including Carrick-on-Suir, Kilsheelan and Mothel. In 1679 he became Dean of Waterford. He died in 1685. He left behind an excellent description of Waterford City and County in the late 17th century which he had written for William Molyneux's projected "Natural History of Ireland". Unfortunately, the book was never written as Molyneux abandoned it in the same year that Arthur Stanhope died. Stanhope's descriptions of Waterford remain with Molyneux's papers in Trinity College Library, Dublin.

STERLING, EDWARD, (1773-1847) Journalist. Born in Waterford and educated at Trinity College, Dublin, and the Irish Bar. He joined the Yeomanry and fought against the Rebels in the Rising of '98. In 1811 he issued a pamphlet on "Military Reform" and became a correspondent of the *London Times* until 1815 when he became a full time member of the staff. He retired in 1840.

STEWART, LOUIS (b.1944) International Jazz Guitarist. Born at Airmount nursing home, Waterford on Jan 5th 1944, he was educated at Synge Street CBS and the College of Technology, Kevin Street, Dublin. He taught himself to play guitar and at the age of 24 he joined the Tubby Hayes Quartet and big band. From 1967 to 1971 he toured Europe three times with the Benny Goodman Orchestra. He has played with Ronnie Scott on many occasions, both in his Soho club and on European and Australian tours. Has played with the George Shearing Trio since 1980. Although his work takes him mainly around Europe, he resides in Dublin and plays there whenever possible. Has made many albums and CDs, recording with famous bands, and was commissioned by the Arts Council to write a jazz suite, "Joycenotes" (1982) first performed at the Cork International Jazz Festival. He has received several awards at the Montreux Jazz Festival, including the Grand Prix (1969) as best soloist. He also received the award as best soloist at the Nordring Radio Festival in 1980. In 1998 he was awarded a Doctorate of Music by Trinity College, Dublin.

STRANGMAN. A name which can be traced back to the 11th century and which has Waterford connections since the 18th century . The firm of Strangman, Courtney & Ridgway was founded in Waterford in 1774, but Joshua Strangman's grandson Henry Ridgway had become sole proprietor by 1801. They owned 6 sailing ships and were actively involved in the Newfoundland trade as well as exporting butter and provisions to England and Portugal. (Ref. R.S. Harrison) In 1787 a Jos. Strangman was a member of a group appointed by the mayor to re-establish the Waterford Chamber of Commerce. Joseph and Thomas Strangman were part of the Quaker group assigned, in October 1797, to purchase at auction, the property which is now Newtown School (but then belonged to Thomas Wyse). In 1793 a Thomas Strangman was on the committee of investors in Samuel Cox's bridge over the Suir. Around 1850 Joseph Strangman Richardson (1816-1870) began a bacon factory at Mary Street, Waterford which became very successful. In 1864 he built a large new factory at Morgan street, on what was then a cabbage field, which was completed on May 24th of that year. As this was the Queens birthday, the factory was known thereafter as The Queen's Bacon Stores. The factory remained in business well into the 20th Century. In the eighteen-nineties it had a capacity of 3,500 pigs per week, with the average kill being 2,000 animals per week. Every side of Bacon produced was stamped "Richardson, Waterford".

STRANGMAN, MARY SOMERVIlLLE (b. 1872) A daughter of Thomas and Sarah Strangman of Carrigmore, Waterford, she qualified as a doctor and practiced in Waterford. She was the first woman to be elected to Waterford Corporation (1912). She was also a member of the Munster Women's Franchise League. During the Civil War in 1922 she helped evacuate the Cork children who were attending Newtown School (and their luggage) to Kilmacthomas, crossing the Free State and the Republican lines en route, so that they could get the train to Cork.

STRANGMAN, WILLIAM (fl.1792)   In 1792 the Waterford papers announced that " William Strangman and Company inform their friends and the public that they have begun the Strong Ale and Beer brewing". They may in fact have taken over an existing brewery on their site at Mary Street. In 1872 the firm became "Davis, Strangman & Co.", and carried on brewing for another seventy years. By the end of the Second World War their business had been declining for some years and in 1955 Guinness took over the Mary Street brewery where brewing of beers under various labels (Cherry's No.1, Phoenix Ale, Smithwick's Ale, Hoffman's) has continued up to the present day.

STRONGBOW, RICHARD FITZGILBERT de CLARE (fl. 1170) Earl of Pembroke. By the beginning of the 12th Century, most of Wales was subdued under the fuedal yoke of Norman barons but there were still conquests to be made. In 1109 Henry 1 of England granted to the Norman, Gilbert de Clare, "all the land of Cardigan, if he could win it from the Welsh". Win it he did, and Pembrokeshire and Glamorgan were soon 'planted' with Normans, Saxons and retired Welsh and Flemish soldiers. The Welsh natives rebelled from time to time and in 1136 killed Gilbert's son, Richard, in battle. Richard's younger brother, also a Gilbert, was made Earl of Pembroke in 1138 and once again crushed the Welsh, a process which was completed by his son, Richard FitzGilbert de Clare, also called Strongbow. He was one of an elite band of young, strong, aristocratic men with Welsh celtic blood in their veins and several generations of colonial experience. Many of these men, who looked across the Irish Sea for opportunities for conquest in the 12th Century, had surprisingly familiar names. Maurice Fitzgerald was the first, followed by the Barrys, the Carews, the Prendergasts and the de Courcys. When, in 1166, one hundred years after the Norman conquest of England, King Dermot Mac Murrough found himself being squeezed out of his kingdom of Leinster, he sailed to England with his beautiful daughter Eva, and obtained permission from King Henry to recruit a champion to fight his cause. He approached and won over Strongbow with the promise of Eva's hand in marriage and the future succession to the throne of Leinster. This action was to begin seven hundred years of foreign domination for Ireland. Over the next four years small groups of professional soldiers trickled over the Irish Sea. On August 23rd 1170 Strongbow arrived with his bride and one thousand men-at-arms. They landed near Waterford, probably at Passage, were joined by King Dermot, and quickly captured the city. The Danish lord of the city, Sitric, was beheaded, and shortly afterwards Stronbow and Eva were married in the city cathedral. Dermot then went on to capture Dublin with his Normans, forcing the Ostman leader Asgall to flee, and was considering the High Kingship when he died suddenly at Ferns. Strongbow was now king of Leinster, but had to fight battles against the High King and a vengful Asgall who returned with a thousand vikings led by John 'the Mad'. Strongbow survived to meet and submit to Henry 11 who arrived in Waterford in October 1171 with 4,000 men – not intent on conquest, but seeking submission from the Norman barons, which he received. He also received homage from the church because it was believed that Pope Adrian had given him the right to govern Ireland, "as a Catholic prince labouring to extend the borders of the church and teach the truth of the Christian faith to a rude and unlettered people". This copperfastened the domination of Ireland for a few hundred years. To assuage Henry's jealousy, Strongbow handed over his conquests and seaports. In 1173 Henry summoned him to his aid in Normandy, and in thanks, returned to him (in1174) the lordship of Leinster.

Strongbow died on June 1st 1176, having just reached middle age, possibly due to an infection in an old wound, and possibly worn out by the frenzy of his mere six years in Ireland. He had one child by Eva MacMurrough, a girl who was named Isabella de Clare, although legend accuses him of slaying a son, by a previous marriage, for cowardice. During his short time in Ireland he amassed an enormous amount of land and property, much of which still bears his name, i.e. Pembroke Road, Pembroke Cottages, the Pembroke Estate etc. A tomb alleged to be his is in Christ Church Cathedral , Dublin. (ref. E. Curtis et al)

SWEENEY, ERIC (b.1948) Composer and head of WIT Music Department. Bórn in Dublin, he was educated at St. Patrick's Cathedral Grammer School; Trinity College, Dublin; and Ulster University. Having worked at RTE, he moved to Waterford RTC in 1981 as Head of Music. He is an active composer and his work includes two symphonies and a number of shorter works. His music has been played at important public concerts in Ireland by amongst others the RTE Symphony Orchestra (including a commission from the GPA piano competition); and in the USA (at the Newport, Rhode Island Music Festival), and France. Under his guidance the Music Department at WIT has acquired a high level of respect. He is also Chairman of the Symphony Club of Waterford, and organist at Christ Church Cathedral. He lives at Summerville Avenue.

SWIFT, BRIAN (b.1952) Mayor of Waterford. Born in Waterford, the only son of Laurence and Teresa (neé Shelly) Swift, he was educated at Mount Sion CBS, UCC and the Law Society (where he qualified as a solicitor). He was first elected to Waterford Corporation in 1979 and has been returned in every subsequent municipal election with the exception of 1991. He was elected to Dáil Éireann in 1987 and served as a TD until May 25th 1989. He was elected Mayor of Waterford in 1986 and in 1998. He has been instrumental, with the support of others, in the introduction of a points system to regulate the allocation of local authority housing in Waterford city. Apart from his service as a TD and a period as a lecturer in Waterford Regional

College, he has practised as a solicitor from 1976 to date, firstly with the late Desmond Counahan, and subsequently in his own firm.

SWIFT, JACK (fl.1960) Born in Waterford, he was the founder (in the Fifties) of Swifts Furniture Factory, of New Street, Waterford, where he was joined by his three brothers, Laurence, Paudie and Liam. The factory, at the height of its production, employed about fifty people. The furniture it produced was of a high quality and was eagerly sought after by Waterford householders. In the Sixties, the firm signed a contract to produce television cabinets for a well-known television manufacturer. Although initially beneficial, too much reliance was placed on this contract, which, when cancelled, led to a decline in the profitability of the firm. In the Eighties, Eddie Kearns became the main shareholder. The factory premises eventually became the art department of Waterford Regional College.

T

THACKERAY, WILLIAM MAKEPEACE (1811-1863) The famous English traveller and writer visited Waterford in 1842 and his comments (recorded in "An Irish Sketchbook") included: "The view of the town, from the bridge and the heights above it, is very imposing, as is the river both ways. Very large vessels sail up almost to the doors of the houses, and the quays are flanked by tall red warehouses, that look at a distance as if a world of business might be doing within them. But as you get into the place, not a soul is there to greet you except the usual society of beggars, and a sailor or two, or a green-coated policeman sauntering down the broad pavement... Poor patched-windowed, mouldy-looking shops form the basement storey of most of the houses;...In one of the streets leading from the quay is a large dingy Catholic chapel of some pretensions,... but a much finer ornament to the church than any of the questionable gewgaws which adorned the ceiling was the piety, stern, simple, and unaffected, of the people within".

TREACY, JOHN (b.1957) Champion athlete. Born in Dungarvan and raised in Villierstown, Co. Waterford. He won the World Cross-Country Championship in Glasgow in 1978 and the same event in Limerick in 1979. Has set Irish track records from 3000 to 20,000 metres and was European junior silver medalist in the 5,000 metres in 1979. He placed seventh in the 1980 Moscow Olympics but won the Silver Medal in the 1984 Los Angeles Olympics. He came first in the 1992 Los Angeles Marathon and first in the 1993 Dublin Marathon. He ran his fastest time (2:09:15) in the Boston Marathon in which he came third. He also came third in the New York Marathon of 1988 and second in Tokyo in1990. He is the first athlete to receive the freedom of the city of Waterford.

TRITSCHLER. The Tritchlers were one of a number of families from the Black Forest region of Germany (which was mainly

Catholic) to leave their homeland towards the end of the nineteenth century, possibly due to the unrest caused by the Franco-Prussian war and the upheavals which presaged the new German Empire. Many feared the jingoism of Bismarck who regarded Catholics as enemies of the state. Like the Heines, they came to Waterford and opened a clockmakers shop on the Mall.   In the nineteen-thirties they moved to the 129 Quay, where, until quite recent times, Paul, George and the late Bobby Tritschler provided a first class jewellery and clockmaking service. Although no longer in the traditional business, the family has grown in Waterford and the different branches now provide services as architects, quantity surveyors and florists. Robin Tritschler (b. 1978), a fifth generation Tritschler in Ireland, is an extremely promising classical singer, still in training, who has often delighted listeners to RTE, and has won a John McCormack award.

U

USSHER, R. J. (1841-1913) Ornithologist. Richard John Ussher was from Cappagh in Co. Waterford. He lived abroad for many years but sometime after 1866 he returned to Ireland and settled down at his father's house at Cappagh. His first great interest was the rather destructive one of egg-collecting, which he pursued enthusiastically for several years before becoming a member of the Irish Society for the Protection of Birds. He then became equally enthusiastic in learning the habits and whereabouts of rare species. This led to the study of avian fossils, stimulated by the discovery, near his own house, of an "ossiferous cavern" which contained the ancient remains of birds. For the last twenty years of his life, he spent much time and money laboriously excavating caves in counties Cork, Waterford, Clare and Sligo to add to our knowledge of extinct fauna. He also spent much time digging in the Sandhills at Tramore, where he is believed to have found many remains of the Great Auk (extinct by 1844) in kitchen middens there. The last one to be seen in this country was found off Ballymacaw in 1834 by a fisherman called Kirby, who captured it by luring it with tid-bits. He sold it to Francis Davis and it was kept in captivity by one of the Goffs of Horetown but died after a few months. Its stuffed body is preserved in Trinity College, Dublin, the only specimen of its kind in this country. Ussher was the principle author (with Warren) of "Birds of Ireland" published in 1906, which remains an important reference book. (Ref. Robert Lloyd Praeger)

V

VAN EESBECK. A family, thought to be of Flemish origins, which settled in Waterford and Cork in the 18th century.

Van ESBECK, EDMUND (b. 1932) Sports writer and author. Born at Tramore, Co. Waterford, on April 18th 1932. He is the son of Louis Van Eesbeck, who was managing director of McCullough's Ironmongers on the Quay, but one 'e' was dropped from his name on his birth certificate in error. Educated in Dublin, he worked for ten years for the *Exchange Telegraph* newspaper (London), and then for thirty years wrote a highly respected column as rugby correspondent for *The Irish Times*. He has written a number of books, including; "100 Years of Irish Rugby" (1975), a biography of W.J. McBride (1976), "The Story of Irish Rugby" (1986) and histories of Cork Constitution and Old Wesley.

VILLIERS-STUART. Mr and Mrs James Henry Villiers-Stuart are the present residents at Dromana, Co. Waterford. When their children were born, they were the 21st generation of the family to occupy that ancient and historical place, perched high on the banks of the River Blackwater, with incredibly beautiful views which are said to have changed little since Sir Walter Raleigh visited the old castle in the 16th century. In 1824, the Rev R. H. Ryland praised "the projecting windows of the castle, the hanging gardens and the beautiful windings of the stream". The original castle was a Desmond stronghold, thought to have been built in the reign of King John, and which came into the Fitzgerald family in the 13th century. In 1457 Gerald Fitzgerald inherited Dromana Castle. His grandaughter, Katherine, became the famous old Countess of Desmond reputed to have been 140 years old at the time of her death in 1604 , when she fell from a cherry tree planted by Sir Walter Raleigh. In 1664, John Fitzgerald, Lord of Decies, died leaving his estate to his daughter and only child, Catherine. She married Edward

Villiers, eldest son of Viscount Grandison, and their son, John Villiers, became Earl of Grandison in 1721. In the course of time, the earl's grandson, George, succeeded to the title. He enjoyed a high standard of living, (his venison was described as the best in the country) and gambled away much of his inheritance, dying without a male heir. His only daughter, Gertrude, married Lord Henry Stuart, the fifth son of the Marquis of Bute, and the family name has been Villiers-Stuart ever since. The old castle had been badly damaged in the wars from 1642 to 1647 and at some stage was largely demolished and replaced by a relatively small Jacobean house which used the dungeons of the castle for its cellars. Towards the end of the eighteenth century, a large Georgian house was built immediately in front of this house. Henry Villiers-Stuart, (1803-1874) was married in 1826. As a surprise for the returning newly-weds, a Hindu-Gothic gateway made of wood was erected at the bridge over the Finisk River. The young couple liked it so much that they had it reconstructed in more permanent materials and used it as a gate-lodge. In the same year Henry, a Liberal protestant supported by wealthy Catholic merchants such as the Meaghers and the Gallweys, was elected MP in place of Lord George Beresford. In national terms, this electoral victory was an important step towards the Catholic Emancipation Act of 1829. However, many tenants later paid for their temerity when hundreds were evicted by the Beresfords. Henry Villiers-Stuart was created Baron Stuart de Decies in 1830. However, the title became dormant in 1874 (the year of his death) apparently because no evidence of his parents marriage could be found. Henry's son, Henry Windsor Villiers-Stuart (1827-1895), although originally ordained in the church, entered politics in 1873 and was elected MP for Waterford (1873-74 and 1880-85). In 1883 he was sent to Egypt and proved to be an able administrator for the British under the nominal rule of the khedive. He became an enthusiastic Egyptologist and established a small museum at Dromana "full of Egyptian mummies". In the late nineteen-fifties the Georgian house at Dromana was thought to be too difficult to maintain and was destroyed. The seventeenth century house is now the family home.

W

WADDING, LUKE (1588-1657) Born in Waterford on October 16th 1588. Educated in Lisbon and Coimbra, he entered the Franciscan Order in 1607. Ordained in Vizeu, Portugal in 1613, he became president of the Irish College at Salamanca in 1617. He then moved to Rome to act as chaplain to the Spanish Mission sent there in 1618 under the leadership of Anthony a Trejo to promote the doctrine of the Immaculate Conception. He founded St Isidore's Irish College, Rome, in 1625 and the Ludovisian College in 1627. He represented the interests of the Irish Catholic Confederation in Rome and according to some, was the principal instigator of the great rebellion of 1641. Kept aware of events in Ireland through his Jesuit cousins (Luke , Ambrose and Michael Wadding), he persuaded the Pope to send financial aid, as well as arms and military expertise to Ireland. He also advised the Pope to send Archbishop Rinuccini to Ireland as Papal Nuncio, and encouraged the great general, Owen Roe O'Neill, to return to Ireland. His aim was the total restoration of the Catholic Church in Ireland. He was a prolific writer and produced many scholarly works including 'Annales Ordinis Minorum" (1624-1625) − a history of the Franciscan Order in eight volumes; Scriptores Ordinis Minorum (1650), and a critical edition, in twelve volumes, of the works of Johannes Duns Scotus, the 13th-century scholar, fellow Franciscan, and zealous defender of the Immaculate Conception. He died on November 18th 1657, and is buried in St Isidore's Church, Rome.

WADDING, PETER (1580-1644) Born in Waterford, a cousin of Luke Wadding, he was educated at Douai (MA, DD, and LLD). Becoming a Jesuit in 1601, he took up professorships of theology successively at Louvain, Antwerp, Prague, and Gratz. He also published a number of theological works.

WALLACE, William Vincent (1812-1865) Composer and musician, born in Waterford City on March 11th 1812. He showed early musical talent and was organist in Thurles Cathedral at the age of 17. He then worked as a violinist and conductor at the Theatre Royal, Dublin, for a few years before marrying a Miss Kelly and emigrating to Australia in 1835. There, he left his wife and undertook sheepfarming and a succession of various jobs as he travelled through Tasmania and New Zealand, returning to music to earn a living there and in India, Nepal, Kashmir, South America and Mexico. In 1844 he married an American pianist in New York and returned to London the following year. In 1845 he wrote the opera "Maritana", which was received enthusiastically when it opened in Drury Lane on November 15th that year. An international tour followed. In 1860 his opera "Lurline" opened at Covent Garden and was even more successful than "Maritana". Legend has it that he sold this opera for fifty shillings, but an equally unconfirmed story says that he gave the rights to a poverty-stricken stagehand. He wrote several other operas, including "Desert Flower" and "Amber Witch" and other musical works, before illness caused him to move to the Chateau de Bagen, in Haut Garonne, France, in 1864. He died there on October 12th 1865, but is buried in Kensal Green Cemetery, London.

WALSH, DAVY. Soccer Player. Born in Waterford. In the 1940s he played soccer for West Brom and Aston Villa, scoring 131 league goals. He was capped 20 times for Ireland.

WALSH, EDWARD (1805-1850) Poet and hedge-school teacher, born in County Waterford, he collected traditional Irish poetry and stories and contributed to nationalist journals. Working as a national school-teacher in Co. Waterford in 1837-43, he published songs and translations of Irish poetry, 1844-47.

WALSH, EDWARD (1756-1832) Physician and army surgeon born in Waterford. Sent to Glasgow for his education he qualified as a doctor there in 1791. He was subsequently Army surgeon in Ireland (1798), and in Holland (1799). Later, he saw service in Canada, in Iberia (throughout the Penninsular War), and at the Battle of Waterloo. He published poetry and a "Narrative of the Expedition to Holland" (1800).

WALSH, FRANKIE (b.1936) Tireless Mount Sion hurler who captained Waterford in their All-Ireland win over Kilkenny in 1959. He also played in the 1957 and 1963 All-Ireland senior finals and was one of the county's most successful interprovincial players winning five medals between 1957 and 1966.

WALSH, JOHN (1835-1881) Poet. Born on Belleville Park estate, near Cappoquin, where his father was employed as a steward, he attended Cappoquin National School. Having trained as a teacher at Marlborough Street Training College in 1853, he returned to the Blackwater valley and for the rest of his life worked as a teacher and poet. His work appeared in a number of periodicals including *The Nation*, *The Irishman*, *The Irish People*, *The Waterford Citizen* and *The Waterford Star*. In 1872 he was appointed teacher in the National School in Cashel. He died there on February 27th 1881. The poem "Longing" is attributed to him.

WALSH, JOSEPH J. (1906-1992) Newspaper proprietor and editor. Youngest son of Edward Walsh, a former mayor of Waterford (1928-1930), he succeeded his father as proprietor/editor of the *"Munster Express"* newspaper in 1943, a position he held for fifty years, becoming Ireland's longest serving newspaper editor. He was educated at Waterpark College and had hoped to study medicine at university but was persuaded by his parents to join the family newspaper and printing business. In later years he liked to recall how, in the Forties, he was approached by the major political parties to stand for election to the Dail, and how the the Ministry of Education was hinted at, in view of his literary background. He decided however to remain with the family newspaper, and over the next four or five decades saw to it that the *"Munster Express"* was the dominant commercial, if not literary, organ in the south-east. "Smokey Joe", as he was widely known, was a somewhat larger-than-life character who liked to be at the centre of things. According to one observer (journalist John O'Connor) "J.J. tended towards the theatrical and, over the years I came to the conclusion that such behavoir was a unique combination of homespun managerial psychology and a wicked sense of humour". He was much travelled and all his journeys were reported on at length in his newspaper. In 1956 he travelled to Australia to see Ronnie Delaney win an Olympic gold medal, and on his return published a book to commemorate the occasion entitled "Across The World for Sport". He was involved with, and contributed to, many charitable and sports organisations, but was most at home where his would always be the final say. He was Master of the Holy Ghost Hospital and Life President of the Waterford Historical and Literary Society of which he was founder. When he died, he would have been pleased to see that his newspaper described the funeral as "one of the largest seen in Waterford for many years".

WALSH, MICHAEL (d. c.1870) One of the last members of a family firm of boat builders and repairers which operated from the Graving Bank. He lived at number 17 The Quay, and at his death, left funds for the erection of The Michael Walsh Asylum, a home for 18 old ladies. The building, a substantial one, was erected in 1875 at the corner of Manor Street and Manor Hill, and had an oratory for the spiritual well-being of the residents. The building was completely renovated in 1995, and is still serving its original purpose.

WALSH, NICHOLAS (d. 1585) Son of Patrick Walsh (d. 1578) bishop of Ossory and bishop of Waterford. Having studied at Paris, and at Oxford and Cambridge (BA and MA), he was appointed chancellor of St. Patrick's, Dublin, (1571). He was also co-translator with John Kearney of the Irish-language version of the New Testament (1573) He became bishop of Ossory in 1577. He was murdered in 1585.

WALSH, ROBERT (1772-1852) Clergyman and writer. A brother of Edward Walsh (1756-1832) (q.v.), he was born in Waterford and educated at Trinity College (BA 1796). Appointed curate at Finglas, Co. Dublin in 1806, he was embassy chaplain at Constantinople in 1820 and in 1831-35. He received an honorary MD from Aberdeen University and Honorary LLD from TCD. He was also embassy chaplain at St. Petersburg and at Rio de Janeiro, 1828-1831. He was designated rector of Kilbride, Co. Wicklow (1835-39), and of Finglas, 1839-52. He published notes on his travels and (jointly with James Whitelaw) a "History of Dublin" (1818) His son, John Edward Walsh (1816-1869) studied law at Trinity College, became a barrister (1839), and writer (he published "Ireland Sixty Years Ago" in 1847), and eventually attorney-general for Ireland and Master of the Rolls (1866), before dying in Paris three years later.

WALTON, ERNEST THOMAS SINTON (1903-1995) Scientist. Born in Dungarvan, Co. Waterford, and educated at Methodist College, Belfast; Trinity College, Dublin; and Cambridge, where he took his PhD in 1931. Working under Ernest Rutherford in Cambridge, he and John Cockcroft achieved the first transmutation of atomic nuclei by artificially accelerated particles (commonly called "splitting the atom"), in 1932. They received full recognition for this in 1952 when they were awarded the Nobel Prize. The Cockcroft-Walton accelerator, which they invented, is still widely used in nuclear physics. Walton returned to Trinity in 1935 where he was made a fellow, and was appointed Erasmus Smith Professor of Natural and Experimental Philosophy in 1946. He retired from Trinity in 1971 but continued his interest in physics to the end of his life.

WALTON, JULIAN C. (b. 1941) Genealogist and Historian. Spent the first five years of his life near Castletownroche in Co. Cork. The family moved to Tramore in 1946, and following the death of his father, his mother married the Waterford solicitor Harry Kenny (who died in 1973). Julian was educated at Christ Church National School, Tramore; Lambrook School (Berkshire); Radley College (Berks.); Christ Church, Oxford (Mod. Lang. 1962); and University College, Cork (H. Dip in Ed. 1965). He became a Roman Catholic in 1963. After leaving University College, Cork he became a secondary schoolteacher and taught at several schools in England and Ireland, including Sutton Park School, Co. Dublin, where he taught from 1970 to 1990. Originally a teacher of modern languages, from 1983 he specialised in History and was briefly vice-president of the History Teachers Association of Ireland. From 1990 to 1993 he worked with Waterford Heritage Genealogical Centre as, in his own words, " a senior trainee". From 1994 to 1996 he supervised the cleaning, conservation and cataloguing of Waterford Cathedral Library (C. of I.)   He is currently employed in a similar project in University College, Cork.   He has had a lifelong interest in history, particularily Waterford history and genealogy.   He is vice-president of the Irish Genealogical Research Society, and a former editor of the Irish Genealogist (1987-89) and Decies (1991-96).   His publications include a series of articles on the Aylward (1970-77) and Bolton (1987-89) families of Co. Waterford, Waterford testamentary records, and reports of the IGRS Tombstone Sub-Committee; on east Waterford tombstones and on Waterford Cathedral Library. In 1992 he wrote the text of "The Royal Charters of Waterford " for Waterford Corporation. Starting in 1994 he has researched and presented a local history slot on WLR-FM originally entitled "On This Day" and from January 1998 called "A Page from our Past". This programme has become extremely popular and has brought to Waterfordians a great awareness and appreciation of local history.

WARE, JIM   (1908-1983) All-Ireland hurling captain. Born in St. Luke's, Cork, but raised in Waterford where he attended De La Salle College. He was a keen hurler, and went on to become captain of the Waterford team which won this county's first All-Ireland when they defeated Dublin in the final of 1948. He also won a number of Railway Cup medals and captained the Munster team to victory in 1949. His brothers, Charlie, Jack and Murty, were also well-known hurlers, Charlie being the first Waterford man to be picked to play for Munster. Jim Ware spent all his working life as a bookbinder with Harveys of Georges Street, and was responsible for the re-binding of much of the library of St. John's College. He married Alice O'Donnell, a poet and playwright, and they lived at Laurence Terrace, Waterford. Mrs. Ware died in 1998.

WATERFORD, EARL of (died 1453)   Sir John Talbot, Lord Justice of Ireland in 1412 and Lord-Lieutenant, 1414-21, was (according to Debrett's Peerage) "a celebrated warrior and gloriously sustained the cause of Henry VI throughout his French realm". He was captured by Joan of Arc at Patay when his army was defeated but was released by exchange, and returned to the fray. He was created Earl of Shrewsbury (in the peerage of England) in 1442 and Earl of Waterford (peerage of Ireland) in 1446. He was previously Ambassador to France (1443) and served as Lieutenant of the Duchy of Aquitaine in 1453, but died fighting at the battle of Chastillon in the same year. The title is still held by the present Earl of Shrewsbury, but the family have little or no involvement with the city or county of Waterford.

WATT, WILLIAM F. (d. 1973) Businessman and music lover. Although a very successful businessman (he was the major shareholder in Waterford Sack and Bag Co. Ltd), Willie Watt's greatest passion was classical music. In his time, he was regarded as one of Ireland's best tenors, and was one of the first singers to be heard on Radio Eireann in the nineteen-twenties. He was still making occasional broadcasts on Radio Eireann in the 1950s. On 28th May 1942 the Waterford Music Club was founded by him along with Elizabeth Downey, Mrs Ida Stukley O'Reilly, and T. F. H. Bayley. Watt was elected chairman, a position he held for thirty years until his death in 1973. He persuaded Patrick Little, Waterford TD and at that time Minister for Posts and Telegraphs, to become first president of the club. This no doubt encouraged a number of broadcasts made from the Music Club's main venue, the Municipal Theatre. The first vice-president of the club was the city manager, Denis Hegarty. Willie Watt also founded the Waterford Festival Choral Society which was a great achievement in that it brought together all, or almost all, the city church choirs, both Catholic and Protestant. His last home was in Dunmore East, at what is now known as the Candlelight Hotel. The Waterford Music Club continues to be a success. In honour of the club's founder, the first concert each season is entitled "The William F. Watt Memorial Concert".

WELDON, TONY. Singer and DJ . He first became well-known as a singer with the famous Frankie King band at weekly gigs in the Arundel Ballroom and other local venues in the 1950s and '60s. Later he led his own band and acted as MC for a number of functions. He has since become a well-liked DJ on WLR-FM since its foundation.

WEST, JOHN (b. 1942) Champion weightlifter (powerlifting). Born in Tallow, Co. Waterford, and educated at CBS Tramore. As a weightlifter he was three times World Champion, seven times European Master Champion, and twelve times British champion. He is a holder of ten records, some of which are still unbroken, and was twice awarded the Aer Lingus Sportsman award. (Ref. *Munster Express*)

WEST, ROBERT (d. 1770) Painter. Born in Waterford, the son of a city alderman. Having studied under Boucher and Vanloo on the Continent, he established a drawing and painting school in Georges Lane, Dublin in 1747. In 1757, the Dublin Society (later, the Royal Dublin Society), set up the Dublin Society School of Art and engaged Robert West to run it. His role as headmaster and particularly as teacher was a great success in spite of the fact that in later years he suffered from severe mental illness. On his death, the headmastership of the school was taken over by his son, Francis Robert West (1749-1809), and in due course by his grandson, Robert Lucius West (d.1849), a painter of portraits and historical subjects. The three Wests taught in the school for a total of 95 years. A measure of the importance of this school can be gauged by the names of some of the famous artists who attended, including: Robert Healy, Charles Forrest, Thomas Sautelle Roberts, George Grattan, James George Oben and John Henry Campbell.

WESTCOTT-PITT, ARTHUR (1899-1979) Businessman and amateur pilot. Was a member of a well-known merchant family which had the agency for the distribution of Tate & Lyle sugar in the south of Ireland. The family built a substantial residence in Dunmore East (in more recent times occupied by the O'Dwyer family) at the beginning of this century, and were share-holders in the now defunct firm of Henry Bell & Co, Chemists, which had a large distinctive sign in the shape of a bell on the Quay beside the Granville Hotel. Arthur was also a private pilot (having been trained by Sir Alan Cobham) and had his own plane, an Austin Autocrat, which he used to fly from a grass runway at Coxtown, Dunmore East (sometimes referred to as "Dunmore East Aerodrome"). He gave almost 30 years service to the Dunmore East Lifeboat, of which he was honorary secretary for twenty- three years, often flying out over the sea in stormy weather to find a boat in distress and direct the lifeboat to it. On occasion he joined the crew of the lifeboat and one rescue earned him three broken ribs and a bronze medal service certificate. At the end of his service he was awarded the rare, gold badge. He was also a representative of the Shipwrecked Fishermen's and Mariners' Royal Benevolent Society for thirty years, and an examiner (for South-East Ireland), of the Royal Lifesaving Society.

He changed his name from Pitt to Westcott-Pitt by deed poll when he married a descendant of Captain George B. Westcott RN, a naval officer under Nelson, who died in action while commanding HMS "*Majestic*" at the Battle of the Nile in 1798.

WHELAN, Bigadier "PAX" (fl.1922) of Dungarvan Co. Waterford, was in overall command of the Decies (West Waterford) Brigade of the IRA. During the Easter Rebellion, he, along with P. O'Mahony and George Lennon, occupied the Dungarvan Post Office. In 1920 the brigade was in action at Piltown, Brown's Pike and Ardmore. In July 1922 Whelan was in command of the Republican forces in Waterford and was prepared to defend the city against the Free State troops moving down from Kilkenny. According to John P. Duggan, the Republicans numbered 300 and were armed with rifles, Lewis guns, and Thompson sub-machine guns. The Free State troops numbered between 600 and 700 and were commanded by Col. John T. Prout. They had with them an 18-pounder artillery piece under the command of Commandant Patrick Paul, an experienced soldier who had fought in France and then had led an East Waterford Battalion against the British. Pax Whelan decided to spread his men around the city in small garrisons at strategic points such as the Post Office on the Quay, the Jail at Ballybricken, and the Police barracks at Adelphi Quay, and "sit tight" (Younger). He was aware that his forces were inadequate for the task and had appealed for help to his comrades in Cork and Tipperary. Meanwhile, on July 18th, the Free State troops gathered at the side of the road near Kilmacow and knelt to receive a General Absolution before the attack. Whelan had Redmond Bridge raised and locked in position. Prout and Paul, anxious to avoid heavy losses, had the 18-pounder dragged across Waterford golf course to Mount Misery and from this vantage point set about bombarding the city. In the process they partially demolished Paul's mother's house in Ballybricken, but maintained an accurate fire over open sights in spite of heavy sniper fire from Bilberry Rock and the Post Office. While this was going on people living on the Quay locked themselves in and barricaded their windows against stray bullets. Many ran through the backstreets to the Manor Street train station and took an impromptu holiday in Tramore. That night, under cover of darkness, Free State troops crossed the river by boat and seized the Adelphi Hotel, the Imperial Hotel (both on the site of the present Tower Hotel) the County Club and the Post Office. No sentries had been posted and the occupants were taken by surprise. The bridge was then lowered and more troops streamed across. By mid morning, no help having arrived from Cork or Tipperary, the Republicans had left the city by lorry, leaving the barracks on fire. The seige of Waterford was over. In spite of the expenditure of 36 shells and thousands of bullets there were only nine deaths during the seige, one being a girl of ten. The shelling had demoralised the defenders, but apart from that, there was a lack of willingness on the part of many of the troops on both sides to take life if it could be avoided. Many officers who had been active against the British were simply unwilling to lead their men against fellow Irishmen. Pax Whelan was eventually captured and imprisoned in Mountjoy Jail where he went on hunger-strike. He was eventually released and lived on into old age.

WHITE, THOMAS (1753-1786) Quaker merchant who came from Harristown, near Edenderry, in 1775 and opened a grocery and ship's chandlery on the corner of Thomas Street and King Street (now O'Connell Street).

WHITE, WILLIAM (fl.1820) Son of Thomas White (q.v.). Taking over his father's business in 1799, he expanded it to include imports of sugar, corn and fish and vegetable oils, which were stored at Hanover Street and The Quay. He was also founder of White's shipbuilding yard which was established at Ferrybank circa 1819/20. The historian R. H. Ryland (in his History of

Waterford - 1824) gave William White the credit for being the first to provide proper ship-repairing and ship-building facilities in Waterford. He said "this port laboured under the disadvantage of being one of the worst in Ireland... so much so, that only dire necessity caused any vessels to be repaired here.... These great disadvantages have been completely removed by Mr. White... By a simple combination of wheels, and an inclined plane, vessels of almost any size can with the greatest facility be drawn completely out of the water... and repaired with the greatest ease imaginable. The vessels which have been built at this establishment are much admired for beauty of model and soundness of workmanship". White's yard built many ships ranging in size from 80 to 900 tons. William also added a chemist's counter to the shop on Thomas Street and established a rope-walk near Keane's Road. On his death, his sons George and Albert took over the business. In 1843 the warehouse at Hanover Street was destroyed in a gigantic fire, fueled by the oils stored there. In 1847 the two brothers had a disagreement and split up, Albert taking over the shipyard and George the shop. According to family tradition, Albert did not make a go of the ship-yard, and in 1861 left for Liverpool "under a cloud". George's daughter Lucy married Joseph Grubb of Clonmel, and two of their four grandchildren - Malcolm (d. 1990 aged 87) and Eric Grubb, (d. 1988 aged 83) - spent all their working lives in George White & Sons, O'Connell Street, until the end of the nineteen-eighties, when the building was taken over by Frank English & Co. (ref Patrick Kavanagh & George Gilmour-White)

WHITE, VINCENT (1885-1958) Medical doctor, politician, and mayor of Waterford. Son of Dr Vincent White (1854-1914) and grandson of Dr Vincent White (1809-1883), he was the third in line in the family to provide sterling service as a dispensary doctor in Waterford. He first came to prominence in political circles in 1916/17 when, following the Rising of 1916 he became a leading member of Sinn Fein. He also won praise "for his tireless work among the poor during the influenza epidemic then sweeping Europe" (E.O'Connor) In 1918 he contested a bye-election, but lost it to John Redmond's son Captain Willie Redmond. Captain Redmond held the seat in the later general election that year, making Waterford the only constituency not to elect a Sinn Fein candidate outside of Ulster and TCD. In the 1920 municipal elections Sinn Fein gained control of Waterford Corporation and Dr White was elected mayor. As mayor, he has been described as colourful (McEneaney) and theatrical (O'Connor), and he certainly was different. He did away with a lot of the pomp and circumstances of his office (although throughout his life as a doctor he dressed formally each day and always wore white gloves) and loved dramatic statements in political life. In 1920, during a two-day general strike to protest against the deregulation of food prices, he gave over the City Hall to "three 'soviet' Commisioners" and allowed them to fly a red flag from the building (O'Connor). In the 1922 general election, White came top of the poll but lost his seat in 1923 whilst campaigning for the Cumann na nGaedheal party of which he was now a member. In the meantime he retained the office of mayor until 1926. He was elected to the Dáil in the 1927 June election, and again in the September election of that year. In 1932 he shared the Cumann na nGaedheal ticket with Willie Redmond and lost his seat. He ran for the Dáil on one more occasion (1933) but failed to be elected. He walked in the St Patrick's Day parade nearly every year until the end of his life, wearing a silk top hat and a black, long-tailed formal coat with an enormous 'barth' of shamrock (the size of which would be argued over for days afterwards) pinned to his breast.

WHITTLE, STEPHEN (b. 1929) Fisherman and lifeboat coxswain. Described (in 1980) as Ireland's most-decorated serving lifeboatman, Stephen Whittle was born in Portally, Dunmore East, and educated at Killea National School. He started fishing with his uncles, often getting up at 4 am to spend a few hours fishing before he went to school. As a young man he went away to join the Merchant Navy and spent six years as a deep sea sailor. He returned to Dunmore to begin fishing again, and in 1959 joined the lifeboat crew. In 1964 he was made second coxswain and in March of that year was awarded his first bronze medal when the lifeboat went to the rescue of the crew of the Dutch coaster "Jan Brons" which had run aground at Ardnamult Head in a south-westerly gale. At great personal risk, Stephen and John Power manned the small boarding boat to span the gap between the lifeboat and the coaster. With the aid of a breeches buoy, they pulled six men, one by one, over the boarding boat to the lifeboat. Bronze medals for seamanship and courage were awarded to the Coxswain, Paddy Billy Power, and to Stephen Whittle and John Power. In 1966 Stephen became Coxswain, and on a dark November night in 1970 was awarded the silver medal for the rescue, in atrocious conditions, of three men from the trawler, *"Glenmalure"*, which was being driven on to Hook Head, having already been wrecked by the sea. Only split-second timing and skillfull seamanship saved the three men. One man, who had been swept from the trawler before the lifeboat arrived, was never found, although Stephen and his crew searched the area for two hours. In 1975 Dunmore was equipped with the new Waveny Class lifeboat, the *"St. Patrick"*, which was a great leap forward in technology. The previous Watson and Barnett class lifeboat had a top speed of only 8 or 9 knots, about half the speed of the *"St. Patrick"* (which would serve the Dunmore East station until 1997). In the same year the *"St. Patrick"* rescued the crew of the collier, *"Michael"*, which was being blown into Tramore bay by Force 11 winds. In July, 1976, a salmon punt being fished by two young brothers from Dunmore was washed onto the Falskirt Rock and capsized. The lifeboat was called but when it arrived only one survivor clung to the upturned boat inside a narrow cove under the cliffs. In a rising south-westerly gale, amongst nets and lobsterpots, Stephen Whittle manouvered the lifeboat within reach (with a lifebuoy), of the 16-year-old. In spite of searching for six hours the body of the other young lad was not recovered that night. Stephen was awarded a second bronze medal for this service. He retired from the lifeboat service in 1984, and lives in the village of Dunmore East with his wife and family.

WIDGER, THOMAS. Was the founder (c. 1860) of the great horse-dealing dynasty and family that still exists to-day. Over a period of thirty years he built up a horse business that was second to none in the then United Kingdom. A newspaper of the 1890s (*"Commercial Waterford"*) reports that, "Messrs. Widger execute heavy commissions for the English, Dutch and Italian governments, and for the nobility and gentry of the United Kingdom, and are large dealers on their own account in various classes of horses, including hunters, race horses, troopers, carriage horses, hacks, etc., of which upwards of 2000 pass annually through their hands". Another source (D. Griffin) indicates that "they were amongst the largest suppliers of cavalry horses in Europe and shipped as much as 200 horses per week out of Waterford Port". At the end of the last century, when horsepower was the only form of transport, they had a number of yards in various locations about the city, including Railway Square, Newgate Street, Mayor's Walk and Keane's Road, backed up by substantial farmlands. They successfully bred racehorses, reaching fourth place in three Grand Nationals before winning that race in 1895 with "Wild Man of Borneo". Thomas Jr, Joseph, Richard and John Widger were all successful racehorse owners in the 1890s. Jack Widger (b.1884), started his career at five years of age, riding in a four and a half mile drag-hunt, and went on to win races when he was barely a teenager. Other Widgers have made their name in racing down through the years, and just a few years ago it was remarked that most of the followers of the Woodstown Harriers seemed to be "young Widgers".

WIGHAM, MAURICE (1918-1998) Headmaster of Newtown School, 1961 to 1978. Born in Monkstown, Co. Dublin, and attended Newtown School from the age of ten to fourteen, completing his secondary education at York. Having obtained a BA in Education and a degree in agricultural science, he taught at St Columba's College, Rathfarnham, for a number of years before joining the teaching staff at Newtown in 1956. He was made Head-master in 1961 and retired in 1978. He married Anna Jacob, who had been a classmate of his at Newtown as a child. He published "The Story of Irish Quakers" in 1992. He died on Jan 2nd 1998, shortly before his book, "Newtown School Waterford, A History" was published.

WYSE, Sir THOMAS (1791-1862) Politician and diplomat, he was born at the Manor of St John, outside Waterford. As a young child he lived at Newtown House (now Newtown School) which had been built for the Wyse family by John Roberts. He was educated at Stonyhurst ('the Catholic Eton') in England; at Trinity College, Dublin (BA, 1812); and at Lincoln's Inn. He travelled extensively in Europe where he met and married

(1821) Laetitia Bonaparte, a niece of Napoleon, but the marriage was not a success and they parted in 1828 never to meet again. He devoted much of his life to the Catholic Emancipation movement, and is described by Roy Foster as the strategist behind the election of the liberal Protestant, Henry Villiers-Stuart, in 1826, and one of O'Connell's main tacticians who encouraged the enlisting of the forty-shilling freeholders in Clare in 1828. He was MP for Tipperary in 1830 and MP for Waterford from 1835 to 1847. He had a particular interest in education, and in 1830, called for Catholics and Protestants to be educated in the same school, the object being "to prepare future citizens for a common country". He was the instigator of many reforms in the education system. In 1835 he introduced a bill for National Education in Ireland, and in 1837 published "Education Reform". He was a lord of the Treasury from 1839 to 1841, and held a number of government positions before being appointed British Ambassador to Greece in 1849. He was knighted and made envoy-extraordinary in 1857 for his successful management of Greek affairs during the Crimean War. He wrote several books including "Walks in Rome" and "Oriental Sketches". He died in Athens in 1862.

WYMBERRY, EDDIE   Comedian, broadcaster and master of ceremonies, he has entertained and amused Waterford audiences for over thirty years, whether it be on the stage or on the air. In the Sixties he was a popular comedian in the Theatre Royal, Waterford. In the Eighties and Nineties his voice has been familiar on WLR-FM where he hosts a popular programme. He was described by the late Sean Dunne as "as much part of Waterford as Reginald's Tower". He specialises in promoting and reproducing the talk and humour unique to Waterford. He has produced two books about local history and humour entitled "Well!" and "Well, Well!".

Y

YOUNG, ARTHUR (1741-1820) English agriculturist and author. Visited Ireland in 1776-79 and published his findings in "A Tour of Ireland". He stayed with Cornelius Bolton at Ballycanvan, and of Waterford he said: "The finest object in this city is the quay, which is unrivalled by any I have seen; it is an English mile long, the buildings on it are only common houses, but the river is near a mile over, flows up to the town in one noble reach, and the opposite shore a bold hill, which rises immediately from the water to a height that renders the whole magnificient.... The Newfoundland trade is the staple of the place... ships go loaded with pork, beef, butter, and some salt, and bring home passengers...or what freights they can, sometimes rum.... The number of people who go passengers to Newfoundland is amazing.... 3000 to 5000 annually, in 60 to 80 ships - they come from most parts of Ireland, and in a year an industrious man will bring home £12 to £16 with him, and some more. There is a foundry at Waterford for pots, kettles, weights, and all common utensils; and a manufactory of anvils to anchors, etc., which employs 40 hands. There are two sugar-houses, and many salt-houses".

A Select Bibliography

Anderson, Ernest B. "Sailing Ships of Ireland", Morris & Co., Dublin 1932.

Arnold, Bruce. "A Concise History of Irish Art" Thames & Hudson, London 1977.

Boylan, Henry, "A Dictionary of Irish Biography", Gill & Macmillan, Dublin 1978.

Browne, Noel, "Against the Tide" , Gill & Macmillan, Dublin 1986.

Browne, Vincent with Michael Farrell, "The Magill Book of Irish Politics", Magill Publications Ltd. Dublin 1981.

Burtchaell, Jack, "Waterford Two Centuries Ago" Decies No 47 Spring 1993.

Butler, Matthew, "A History of the Barony of Gaultier" Downey & Co., Waterford, 1913.

Cavanagh, Michael, "Memoirs of Thomas Francis Meagher" Messenger Press, Mass. USA 1892.

Cowman, Des, "Landlords and their Minerals c. 1850" Decies No 47 Spring 1993.

Cousin, John W. and D. C. Browning, "Dictionary of Literary Biography" Pan Books , London 1969.

Crone, J. S., "A Concise Dictionary of Irish Biography", Talbot Press. Dublin 1937.

Curtis, Edmund, "A History of Ireland", Methuen & Co. Dublin 1936.

Dalton, Fr William, "The Amazing History of Ferrybank Church", article in The Munster Express, Jan. 3rd 1997, p.22

Davis-Goff, Annabel, "Walled Gardens", Barrie & Jenkins, London 1990.

de Breffny, Brian, and Rosemary ffolliott, "The Houses of Ireland" Thames & Hudson, London 1975.

Debrett's Peerage, Baronetage and Knightage, Dean & Son. London 1905.

de Courcy, Catherine, & Maher, Ann. "Fifty Views of Ireland". The National Gallery. Dublin 1985

de Courcy, John, "The History of the Waterford Music Club".

Dowling, Daniel, "Waterford Streets Past and Present", Waterford Corporation, Waterford 1998.

Dowling, Daniel & Maurice Hurley, "Housing in Waterford", Waterford Corporation, 1988.

Duggan, John P. "A History of the Irish Army" Gill & Macmillan. Dublin 1991.

Egan, P., "History, Guide and Directory of the County and City of Waterford", Dublin, 1894.

Fewer, Michael G. "By Cliff and Shore", Walking the Waterford Coast. Anna Livia Press. Dublin. 1992.

Fewer, Thomas Gregory, "Poverty and Patronage; responses to the famine on the Duke of Devonshire's Lismore Estate". The Famine In Waterford Des Cowman and Donald Brady, Eds. Waterford. Waterford County Council. 1995.

Fewer, Thomas Gregory, "Land Tenure in South Kilkenny, C. 1800-1850" Unpublished Master of Arts thesis, University College Cork, 1993.

Freeman, Norman, "Classic Hurling Matches 1956 - 1976" Gill & Macmillan, Dublin 1993.

Friel, Maeve, "Here Lies - A guide to Irish Graves" Poolbeg Dublin 1997.

Gillespie, Raymond & Kennedy, Brian P. "Ireland: Art into History", Town House, Dublin 1994.

Gillespie, Frances; Mooney, Kim-Mai, and Ryan, Wanda, "Fifty Irish Drawings and Watercolours". National Gallery of Ireland. Dublin 1986.

Gilmour-White, George, "The Whites of Waterford" a private paper, 1978.

Gray, Tony, "Ireland This Century", Little, Brown & Co., London 1994.

Griffith, Arthur, (ed.) "Meagher of the Sword", M.H. Gill & Son, Dublin, 1916.

Griffin, D. "A Parcel from the Past", Intacta Print Ltd., Waterford 1994.

Hallinan, Michael, "Tales from the Deise", Kincora Press, Dublin 1996.

Hansard, Joseph, "The History, Topography and Antiquities (Natural and Ecclesiastical)...of the County and City of Waterford" Jos. Hansard Dungarvan 1870.

Harrison, Richard S., "A Biographical Dictionary of Irish Quakers", Four Courts Press Ltd., Dublin, 1997.

Hayes, Richard, "Biographical Dictionary of Irishmen in France" M. H. Gill & Son, Dublin, 1949.

Hearne, John M., "The Phoenix Arises: The Early Years of Waterford Glass", Decies No 50, 1994.

Heron, Marianne, "The Hidden Gardens of Ireland" Gill & Macmillan. Dublin 1993.

Hyman, Louis, "Jews in Ireland", Irish University Press, Dublin 1972.

Inglis, Henry David, "Ireland in 1834", London 1834.

Irish, Bill, "Ship-building in Waterford", article in Decies 46 - 1992.

Jones, Paul, "The Irish Brigade" The New English Library, New York, 1969.

Kavanagh, Patrick, "Rope-Making in Waterford", article in Decies 52, 1996.

Keogh, Daire, "Edmund Rice 1762 - 1844", Four Courts Press, Blackrock, Co. Dublin, 1996.

Keogh, Daire, "Thomas Hussey, Bishop of Waterford and Lismore, 1797-1803, and the Rebellion of 1798" in Waterford History & Society, William Nolan and Thomas P. Power, eds., Geography Publications, Dublin 1992.

Killanin, Lord, and Duignan, Michael V., "The Shell Guide To Ireland", The Elbury Press, London. 1962.

Lahert, Richard, "Some Charitable Institutions of Old Waterford", Decies 28 - 1985.

MacCormack, Danny, "The Waterford Hero", The Waterford Post, December 1994.

McCann, Owen, "Greats of Gaelic Games", Gaelic Publications, Dublin 1980.

McCarthy, Michael J.F., "Five Years in Ireland". Hodges, Figgis & Co., Dublin, 1903.

McElwee, Richard, "The Last Voyages of the Waterford Steamers", Intacta Print, Waterford, 1992

McEneaney, Eamonn, (Ed.) "A History of Waterford and its Mayors from the 12th to the 20th Century", Waterford Corporation, Waterford 1995.

McGovern, W.G., "Waterford Crystal Glass",1978.

McRedmond, Louis, (Ed.) "Modern Irish Lives - A Dictionary of 20th-Century Biography", Gill & Macmillan, Dublin 1996.

McVeagh, John, Editor, "Richard Pococke's Irish Tours", Irish Academic Press, Dublin 1995

Morris, Henry, F. "The Principle Inhabitants of County Waterford in 1746", in 'Waterford History & Society", William Nolan & Thomas P. Power eds. Geography Publications, Dublin,1992.

Murphy, Sean & Sile, "The Comeraghs" Comeragh Publications 1996.

Nolan, William & Power, Thomas P. (Eds.) and D. Cowman (Assoc. Ed.), "Waterford History and Society", Interdisciplinary Essays on the History of an Irish County, Geography Publications, Dublin 1992.

Oaksey, John, "Oaksey on Racing" The Kingswood Press, London 1991.

O'Connor, Emmet, "A Labour History of Waterford", Waterford Trades Union Council, Waterford 1989.

O'Connor, John, "The Munster, the Music and the Village", The Munster Express, Waterford, 1996.

O'Connor, Peter, "A Soldier of Liberty" Recollections of a socialist and anti-fascist fighter. MSF Dublin 1996.

O'Doherty, Martina Ann, "Teresa Deevy, Playwright (1894 - 1963)", in Decies 51 - 1995.

O'Faillon, Paraic, "Who's Who in the Irish War of Independence and Civil War, 1916-1923" Dublin 1980.

O'Rourke, Fergus J., "The Fauna of Ireland", The Mercier Press, Cork, 1970.

O'Shea, Ken (Ed.), "Who's Who in Waterford", Tribune Newspapers plc 1994

Parker, Peter (Ed.), & Kermode, Frank (Con. Ed.), "The Reader's Companion to 20th-Century Writers", Fourth Estate Limited, London 1995.

Power, Dermot, "A History of the Peoples Park" in Decies No. 52 - 1996.

Power, Very Rev. Canon Patrick, "The Place-Names of Decies", Cork University Press, Cork, 1952.

Power, Patrick C., "History of Waterford City and County", Mercier Press, 1990.

Praeger, Robert Lloyd, "Some Irish Naturalists" Dublin, 1949.

Smith, Raymond, "The Hurling Immortals", Aherlow Publishing, Dublin 1984.

Somerville-Large, Peter, "The Irish Country House - A Social History", Sinclair-Stevenson, London 1995.

Spry, M. Irene, "The Palliser Expedition", The Macmillan Co. Toronto, 1963.

Thackeray, William Makepeace, "The Irish Sketchbook", London 1843.

Wallace, Martin, "100 Irish Lives", David & Charles, London 1983.

Walsh, Nicholas (ed.) with Ann-Marie Wilsdon & Laura Shaw, "Waterford Harbour Sailing Club - a history ". 1994.

Walton, Julian C. "Hubert Gallwey, An Appreciation", The Irish Genealogist 1984.

Walton, Julian C., "Two Descriptions of Waterford in the 1680s" Decies No 35 - Summer 1987.

Wilkinson, Clennell, "Nelson" George G. Harrap & Co. Ltd, London 1931.

Wynne, Michael (Keeper, NGI) "Recent Acquisitions 1980-81", National Gallery of Ireland, Dublin 1981.

Young, Arthur, "Tour in Ireland". London, 1780.

Younger, Carlton, "Ireland's Civil War". Frederick Muller Ltd, London, 1968.

Index